SINNING
LIKE A
CHRISTIAN

WILLIAM H. WILLIMON

SINNING
LIKE A
CHRISTIAN

A NEW LOOK
AT THE
7
DEADLY SINS

Abingdon Press
Nashville

SINNING LIKE A CHRISTIAN
A NEW LOOK AT THE SEVEN DEADLY SINS

This book is printed on acid-free paper.

Library of Congress Cataloging-in-Publication Data

Willimon, William H.
   Sinning like a Christian : a new look at the seven deadly sins / William H. Willimon.
      p.   cm.
   Includes bibliographical references (p.   ).
   ISBN 0-687-49280-7 (binding: pbk. : alk. paper)
1. Deadly sins.   I. Title.

   BV4626.W56 2005
   2418.3—dc22

                                                                    2005012248

ISBN 13: 978-1-4267-5823-2

13 14 15 16 17 18 19 20 21 22—10 9 8 7 6 5 4 3 2 1

MANUFACTURED IN THE UNITED STATES OF AMERICA

To my fellow sinners
in the North Alabama Conference
of The United Methodist Church

CONTENTS

INTRODUCTION

Once there was One who came to us, who touched the untouchables, turned his back upon the world's bright baubles, loved even unto death, and never turned his eyes away from God. And we hated him for it. He came to us with wide open hands in gracious invitation, seeking us, both patient with us and hotly pursuing us. And thereby he brought out the very worst in us.

We figured that things between us and God were not all that bad, but when he spoke to us of God, and ourselves, and rubbed our noses in the filthy rags of our presumed righteousness, well, we thought we were good until we met him. He called upon us to attempt great moral feats, and then watched as we fell flat on our faces. He invited us to join up with his Kingdom, then set that

Kingdom's demands so high that when it came time for us to stand up and show what we were made of, we fled, slithering into the darkness. He said, "Come to me. Take on my yoke." And we with one voice cried, "Crucify him!"

A recent study of young adults' reaction to the church says that right up at the top of twenty- to thirty-somethings' beefs with the church is that "Christians are too judgmental." That is, we talk too much about sin.

I do wonder if people are as dumb as much of mainline, progressive Protestantism—or for that matter, as self-deceptive as allegedly evangelical, biblical conservatism—takes them to be. As C. S. Lewis noted, "It is the policy of the Devil to persuade us there is no Devil."[1] It is a sure sign of a compromised church—a church that has retired from doing battle with the principalities and powers, a church without prophets—when one finds a church that has ceased dealing with sin.[2] Or as a character in one of Oscar Wilde's plays says, "One should believe evil of everyone, until, of course, people are found out to be good. But that requires a great deal of investigation nowadays" (*A Woman of No Importance*).

When I openly marveled at the success of TV's "Dr. Phil," wondering why his Texas-direct, blunt-to-the-point-of-cruel talk got him such an audience, a psychotherapist in my congregation explained, "People are ready to be told the truth about themselves, even when it hurts, because they know that without getting the truth, they won't get life." Even if we don't enjoy having the truth told directly to us, we do enjoy listening in as Dr. Phil tells the truth to someone else.

Anton Chekov, in his *Notebooks*, said that a person "will only become better when you make him see what he is like." And you really haven't told the truth about us until you have told us that down deep, when all is said and done, even at our very best, we sin.

We have even enlisted Jesus into our self-delusion project, reducing even wild-eyed, prophetic, judgmental Jesus into a quivering mass of affirmation and oozing graciousness. Odd, considering how frequently, unguardedly, and gleefully Jesus told us that we were sinners, forgiven to be sure, but still sinners. Anyone who thinks that Jesus was into inclusiveness, self-affirmation, and open-minded, heart-happy acceptance has then got to come up with a reason for why we responded to him by nailing him to a cross. Jesus got nailed not for urging us to "consider the lilies," but for calling us religious leaders "whitewashed tombs," and even worse.

Yet it is perhaps not such a mystery that we have attempted—scripture be damned—to produce a promiscuously permissive, user-friendly Jesus. After all, we are the folk who, having just lived through history's most bloody century, kicked off a new one on a September morn by witnessing the killing scores of innocent civilians, then excusing another Bush war that slaughtered even more innocent civilians in Iraq, followed by a vigorous but ultimately futile Obama war in Afghanistan—all for the very best of democratic, national motives. Let's simply say that we are not off to a particularly good start at presenting ourselves as good, kind, loving, progressive, and enlightened folk who have at last put all that primitive sin behind us.

I asked a recovering alcoholic in my congregation, "Sam, why have you stopped coming to church?" He replied, "Preacher, after you have been to AA, and taken the cure, and stared your demons in the face, and have to stand naked in front of twenty other drunks and tell every bad thing you have done or thought, and had to ask God and them to forgive you for being you, well, church just seems like such a trivial waste of time."

Church is about more than sin, but, by the grace of God, it ought not to be less than this.

It is of the prophetic ministry of the church to teach people that we are sinners. Think of church as lifelong learning in how to be a sinner. We may be conceived in sin, but we have no means of being cognizant of sin without the grace of God. The "sins" of non-Christians tend to be rather paltry. For Christians, sin is not so much inherent in the human condition, though it is that; rather, sin is the problem we have between us and God. It is rebellion against our true Sovereign, an offense against the way the Creator has created us to be. The gospel story that we are forgiven-being-redeemed sinners is the means whereby we are able to be honest about the reality, complexity, persistence, and perversity of our sin.

Many sensitive and thoughtful people are aware of a general disease and disorder in human existence. Read this morning's news, take a course in the history of Western civilization, focus upon the lifestyle of your brother-in-law, sit through a meeting of the United Methodist General Conference, and it will take little imagination to believe that we sin, whether or not you believe Jesus Christ is Lord. This generalized awareness of human finitude has little to do with the Christian notion of sin. Sin is more than taboo, dread, or shame. The Septuagint Bible's translation of "sin" by *hamartia* or "missing the mark" only compounds the confusion. Sin is more than simply not quite living up to our human potential, stumbling, making mistakes, or being off the mark by a notch or two. When Christians refer to sin, we are describing more than the universal cultural phenomenon that human beings screw up and occasionally live as we ought not. Reinhold Niebuhr, citing Herbert Butterfield, is well known for his remark that the doctrine of original sin is the only empirically verifiable Christian doctrine. Even those who do not know that Jesus Christ is Lord know sin.

Niebuhr was wrong. Christian sin results not from our unhappiness with the limits of human existence and our inappropriate response to our discontented finitude (Niebuhr).[3] Rather, Christian sin is derivative of and dependent upon what Christians know about God as revealed in Jesus Christ. We thought we were good people until we met Jesus. Jesus became for us not only a window into the heart of God, but also a mirror held up to us to show us the hard truth about ourselves.

One of the things that impressed me in my reading of the church's classical accounts of the Seven Deadly Sins is the lack of biblical, theological grounding for these accounts, even when they are devised by so great a theologian as St. Thomas Aquinas. I believe that the best reasons why Christians should care about sin are theological rather than anthropological. Something is there in this God who came to us as Jesus Christ that makes us care about an otherwise rather commonplace and all-too-human inclination such as Lust, enables us to name sin's peculiar offense, and enables us to regard that very inclination that contributes to the conception of human life as a matter that is "deadly."

The church's notion of sin, like that of Israel before it, is peculiar. It is derived not from speculation about the universal or general state of humanity, but rather from a peculiar, quite specific account of what God is up to in the world. What God is up to is named as Covenant, Torah, or, for Christians, the Cross of Jesus. If we attempt to begin in Genesis, with Adam and Eve and their alleged "fall," we will be mistaken, as Niebuhr was, into thinking of sin as some innate, indelible glitch in human nature. We must start with Exodus rather than Genesis, with Sinai rather than the Garden of Eden, with Calvary.

Only by getting the story straight—God's story of redemption—are we able to tell our stories truthfully. Christians believe that the only means of understanding our sin with appropriate seriousness and without despair is our knowledge of a God who manages to be both gracious and truthful. Our human situation is not that we are all dressed up with a will to power and lust for transcendence with nowhere to go but frustrating finitude and failure. Our situation is that we view our lives through a set of lies about ourselves, false stories of who we are and who we are meant to be, never getting an accurate picture of ourselves. Through the "lens" of the story of Jesus we are able to see ourselves truthfully and call things by their proper names. Only through the story of the cross of Christ do we see the utter depth and seriousness of our sin. Only through this story that combines cross and resurrection do we see the utter resourcefulness and love of a God who is determined to save sinners (Romans 3:21-25). Thus Barth could claim that "There is no knowledge of sin except in the light of Christ's cross."[4]

In Hieronymus Bosch's painting in the Prado, Madrid, painted around 1485, the Seven are depicted as spokes in a wheel, or rays of the sun. At the center is a large eye, the all-seeing God who knows all our secrets. Yet this is also the God whose nature is holiness and light, who makes the otherwise typical human inclinations to be called sin.

This book, and its reception by the church, has shown me that there is a willingness among many to face the truth about ourselves. While *Sinning Like a Christian* is a work of Christian anthropology—that is, an exploration of who we are as people—in order to be a faithful, peculiarly Christian account, it will need to be theological. We can honestly speak of sin only from the starting point of our redemption, otherwise our talk of sin will either lack seriousness or lead us into idle, perverse curiosity. I therefore agree with Baptist theologian James McClendon when he says that, in order to think rightly about the church's received doctrine of sin,

> it will be necessary to make a starting point, not in Adam's (or Eve's!) alleged act of sin on behalf of innocent babes and faithful believers born an æon later, but rather in the full faithfulness of Jesus of Nazareth, who resisted the temptation that confronted him all the way to his cross, who overcame the principalities and the powers of his day at the price of his life, and who, risen from the dead, summoned followers to abandon every sin and to follow in good faith the pioneer of their salvation. A doctrine of sin linked to this central narrative ... [will not only show] the dark shadow sin casts ... [but will also] hold up this divine faithfulness as the measure of

every life, and it must confess that whatever falls short of, denies, or contradicts Christ's faithfulness is sin."[5]

To witness to that peculiar story is to keep asking for forgiveness for the sin against God that we know and that we do not know. It is to beg, Sunday upon Sunday, for absolution from the sin that is the result of our insidious evil intent, and the sin that is the result simply of our being humans who sometimes screw up. It is to keep living in the faith that Jesus really does intend finally to have the world through the inept ministrations of a bunch of sinners like us.[6] It is to sit lightly on our meager moral triumphs, knowing that they are tinged with more than a touch of sin, and at the same time to be gentle with our and our neighbor's failures, not expecting too much from people like us. It is to have a sense of humor that is born out of our amazement that Jesus Christ died, not for national glory, or a two-car garage, or a fat pension (all those ideals to which we give our lives), but *to save sinners*, that is, people like us. Because of God's peculiar thing for sinners, it is possible for us to confess our sin and still live in faith, hope, and love, knowing that even in our sin we are able to believe that "we are more than conquerors through him who loved us" (Romans 8:37).

So consideration of sin, from a Christian point of view, ought always to begin with, and ought always to keep itself tethered to, the Christ who comes to seek and to save, to share meals with and to redeem, sinners. We also ought to keep in mind that consideration of sin puts us on risky turf. Theologian Karl Barth says that we must take care not to take sin too seriously. Satan must not be honored in any way, especially not honored with our sustained intellectual fascination. Sin is real, pervasive, deadly *but finally defeated*, says Barth. Christ's Adversary still roams, and yet, after the Adversary's defeat on Good Friday and Easter, the Adversary's doom is sure. Thus Barth speaks of sin as *Das Nichtige*—nothingness, pointlessness. It would be theologically perverse to become more captivated and impressed with human sin than we are with divine redemption of our sin.

Self-deceit takes many forms. That I have even taken the trouble to contemplate the Seven Deadly Sins may be an indication that I am attempting to cover my own complicity in sin by taking the initiative, going on the offensive, in a perverse attempt to cover my own sins. I get the jump on you by so honestly naming your sin in order to deflect attention from mine. By naming your sloth, I protect my greed. I will attempt eloquently to argue that my sin in writing this book for money is not as morally meaningful as your failure to get out of bed, sit down at the computer, and write this book. The moral crusader is, at least in literature, frequently the notorious closet pervert.

As noted, Karl Barth warns us against becoming too fascinated with evil and giving evil too much consideration. My fascination with some forms of moral perversity could be, in itself, perverse. My focus on your lust enables me to be a profligate by proxy. Why should not the British have one of the lowest murder rates in the world? They have Agatha Christie, Dorothy Sayers, P. D. James, and all the other great feminine novelists of murder and mayhem. Who needs to commit a sin, when you can vicariously enjoy having it described so well? During my years as chaplain at Duke, more than one aspiring student has noted that I am just a bit too gleeful in my sermonic condemnations of their greed. That I do not make the salaries that they will one day earn is perhaps the source of my righteous indignation. Be careful of a *ménage à trois* among envy, greed, and anger, particularly in church.

Oscar Wilde rebuked all of us moralists and defenders of righteousness by saying, "I never came across anyone in whom the moral sense was dominant who was not heartless, cruel, vindictive, log-stupid, and entirely lacking in the smallest sense of humanity. Moral people, as they are termed, are simple beasts. I would sooner have fifty natural vices than one unnatural virtue." One would of course have expected that of Oscar,[7] still one can understand his sentiments.

It helps, when we speak of sin, to take care always and everywhere to speak of *our* sin, *my* sin. Who better to know sin than those within the household of God? In his *People of the Lie*, Scott Peck says that, if one is looking for genuine evil, then one ought to look first within the synagogue and church.[8] It is the nature of evil to "hide among the good." Satan masquerades as an angel of light. Lucifer is his name, after all. Leaders of the church such as me must beware, not only because we work among the godly, but also because we ourselves, called to speak to and for God to God's people, are in a morally vulnerable position where sin is always lurking about the door (Genesis 4:7).

Another thing to be initially noted about the Seven Deadly Sins is they are all not only so very personal and individual but also so small and trivial. Gluttony, lust, and pride, while not the most attractive of personal attributes, can hardly compete with sexism, racism, and the bloodletting actions of a nation with the largest military budget and the biggest prison population of any people in the world.

The Seven seem so small, so ordinary and unavoidable, compared with so many other sins, and many writers have called them so. Brecht's *Seven Deadly Sins of the Petite Bourgeoisie* is a satire that features two middle-class women searching through seven cities for an appropriately cozy little house to call home. W. H. Auden's "Ode" (1931) calls the Seven "the battalion of Fear," the obsessions of squeamish souls who worry about every little foible as if it were a big deal. James Joyce, in his short story "The Dead," presents the Seven in symbolic form during an unending "purgatorial" evening when Gabriel endures a group of pompous, insipidly pitiful old people.

When we think of "evil," we almost never think of anything within us. Evil is always depicted by us as an impersonal source outside ourselves—tornadoes, floods, earthquakes, and sickness. "The Devil made me do it." Sometimes people say, "With all the suffering and evil in the world, how can I believe in God?" implicating God in our experience of evil. Yet Genesis depicts a primal world that was pleasant, innocent, and idyllic until that day when we arrived. Evil arises with the advent of humanity, not with God's creation of the world. Jesus said that evil arose, not from the way the world is set up, but from what comes up out of the human heart (Mark 7:20-23).

Perhaps that's why it is just a bit easier to lament the evil that is large, systemic, political, natural, and cosmic. Keep sin large, global, universal. Talk about the evil done to us by these wicked institutions, these unjust systems of economic distribution. Surely part of the popularity of the bogus *Left Behind* books is that they posit the threat of evil out there, somewhere, in some vast cosmic conspiracy. Jesus, the one better represented in the New Testament than in the versions of *Left Behind*, might tell us that we don't need to look far to discover the source of most of the bad that afflicts us. Judas betrayed Jesus for nothing more than thirty pieces of silver. The Seven, while sometimes appearing small and trivial in comparison with some of humanity's other sins, at least keep sin personal—your sin, my sin, our sin. Scott Peck says that "the major threats to our survival no longer stem from nature without but from our own human nature within. It is our carelessness, our hostilities, our self-ishness and pride and willful ignorance that endanger the world."[9] G. K. Chesterton was asked by a British newspaper to contribute an essay on the subject "What Is Wrong with the World?" Chesterton sent back a two-sentence essay: What is wrong with the world? *Me*.

Surprised by the church's eager reception of this book, I offer this slightly revised new edition of *Sinning Like a Christian*. This was the first book I wrote after becoming a bishop. What does that tell you? It tells me that, in getting to be a bishop I got a front-row seat to observe (and even to instigate!) some of the most heinous and subtle sin—church sin. It also tells me that one of the joys of being a preacher like a bishop is to be goaded by the gospel of Jesus Christ into telling the truth about us and God.

Thank God that Jesus Christ saves sinners. Only sinners.

William H. Willimon

CHAPTER ONE

THINKING
ABOUT SIN

I n the lurid film *Seven*, starring Morgan Freeman and Brad Pitt, a maniacal killer roams the streets killing a string of victims in a series of gruesome murders. The detectives are stumped until they realize that the perpetrator is killing his victims as a sort of sick punishment for their having committed one of the Seven Deadly Sins. The murders are terrible, the crime scenes are horrible. The whole movie is dark, somber, and sinister.

In other words, the movie is quite unlike the historical depictions of the Seven. If only it were true that these sins were the peculiar provenance of the maniac and the madman, a Hitler or a Mao. But the thing that first impresses us about the Seven is how utterly ordinary and unspectacular they are. These are the mundane, all-too-human foibles of the human race in general, not of the few utterly depraved. Perhaps there is something in us that wants to believe that "sin" must apply to someone other than ourselves. Thus we make a movie that depicts the Seven as lurid, bloody, and spectacularly bad. They are not. This is where we live, this is who we are.

I wrote this book just after having undergone my church's rather laborious process of episcopal election. My experience of that process by which my church chooses its leaders gave me so many opportunities to observe sin in action—the sins of others and my own—that I became interested in this subject afresh. A process of election that leads to clerical exaltation, a process in which nominees are asked positively to present themselves before others while at the same time acting humble and self-effacing about the whole thing, and a process in which electors must make decisions about the suitability and spirituality of the nominees, is a process that is replete with opportunities for sin. Self-delusion is virtually unavoidable in such a situation. At least it was so for me. Shortly thereafter I watched the shenanigans of the candidates in both political parties during a presidential election—their false promises, self-deceit, and misrepresentation—and thought to myself, *mea culpa, mea culpa.*

As a pastor and a Southerner, I've long been fascinated with sin, my own and that of my parishioners. When one sets out to do good things among good people in a good organization, sin is never far away. In my last parish, some years ago, I wrote a book about sin and evil.[1] But that book depicted sin in a rather large, cosmic, systemic manner. I am now, after the election of bishops, more impressed with the rather mundane, ordinary, petty nature of our sin, just the sort of sin that is named in the Seven.

One of the first curiosities about the Seven Deadly Sins is that there are so few sins on the list. Just as God graciously gave us only Ten Commandments, considering all that God might have commanded us, so the church Fathers stopped at a holy, complete number, Seven. They are pride, envy, wrath, sloth, avarice, gluttony, and lechery, or by their more elegant Latin names: *superbia, invidia, ira, acedia, avaritia, gula, luxuria.* For fifteen hundred years the Heptalog has been a Christian way of naming the nature of sin.

The earliest Christian formulation of the Seven is from a contemporary of Augustine, the desert father Evagrius of Pontus in his *Praktikos.* Evagrius was a follower of Origen, who was condemned at the Fifth Ecumenical Council in A.D. 553. In Egypt, Evagrius established a group of monks who went out in the desert to live in order to separate themselves from the wiles of the world and to be closer to God. There is some irony that, out in the desert, in this communal, pure, ascetic community that was designed to promote a better vision of God, Evagrius and his fellow monks discovered their own sin. When Jesus went out into the desert at the beginning of his ministry, there he met Satan, there he was tempted. In the wilderness, alone, sin crouches by the door. Evagrius's *Praktikos* influenced the more famous

3

monastic rule of St. Benedict, which became the means of ordering monastic life in the Western church.

Evagrius's ideas about sin are curious. For instance, he said that women and bishops constituted the greatest temptations to monks, and that both should be avoided as much as possible. He got at least one of those warnings right. His *Praktikos* is a collection of short reflections upon the various aspects of the ascetic life, practical guidelines that make communal life in such close proximity possible. He lists "eight demons" that make life in community, particularly community that is dedicated to God, so difficult.

From time to time we have an earnest little group of seminarians who move out of the dormitory, rent an old rambling house near campus, and set up a "Christian community." Most of these attempts at communal living in Christ do not endure long, as history has shown. Jesus calls us to live with our sisters and brothers in Christ-like family. In these communal attempts, most Christians act exactly like a family—fighting among themselves, full of resentment and envy, and all the rest. So the Seven are the only truthful account that I know of what "family values" really look like. They are the sins that arise most vigorously precisely among those who obey Jesus' command to "love our neighbor" by moving in with our neighbor. I expect the poet Auden was thinking about the difficulty of life in proximity when he quipped that everybody knows we are created to serve our neighbor, but God only knows why the neighbor was created.

The most extensive dissertation on the subject of the Seven was by St. Thomas Aquinas. Aquinas differentiated between the "spiritual sins," like pride, anger, envy, covetousness, and sloth, and the two "carnal sins" of lust and gluttony. I doubt that these sins can be so easily separated. Our body and soul, spiritual and physical, psyche and soma are intertwined. Yet it is probably worth saying that these early Fathers—despite popular misconceptions about Christian sexual prudery, and indeed despite the church's current heated debate over sexual sins—agreed that when it comes to evaluating sin, spiritual sins were decidedly more detrimental and deadly than the carnal.

The first thing that strikes one about the Seven is that they don't seem so "deadly." Why worry about gluttony when murder is so prevalent among us? Surely there are more serious sins than Sloth, Greed, Gluttony, Anger, Lust, Envy, and Pride. The Seven are the stock and trade of daytime soap opera TV, but they are hardly the most terrible things of which human beings are capable. The more spectacular sins—political tyranny, ethnic hatred, religious persecution, and racial violence—fail to make the list. On our campus we are currently terribly concerned with academic dishonesty—cheating—but you won't find it among the Seven. In the churches that I have served, adultery, not to mention drunkenness, is certainly a source of great misery and cruelty. Why not go with adultery, a sin that is so directly, specifically condemned by Jesus, rather than lust? Smoking is one of the most deadly sins in my world, but we learned to inhale rather late in our development, so there's no chance of nicotine making the list. I've seen folk suffer more terribly from alcoholism than from overeating; why not list drunkenness as one of the Seven, rather than gluttony? You've got to question a theology of sin that takes murder less seriously than sloth.

Perhaps this accounts for why most contemporary accounts of the Seven, at least twentieth-century accounts, take them with a large dose of humor, sarcasm, and urbane wittiness, as if troubling oneself over these utterly ubiquitous, human inclinations is evidence of the pitifully hung-up, persnickety church at its most fastidious. It is of the nature of the modern to ridicule and deride any attempt to constrain unrestrained human self-expressiveness.

Gregory the Great gave us the first formal sevenfold division of sin. In his *Morals on the Book of Job* (XXXI, 87), Gregory listed the seven principle vices or "capital sins." Gregory is clear that what makes the Seven so deadly is their generative quality. He says things like, "From envy there springs hatred, whispering, detraction, exaltation at the misfortunes of a neighbor, and affliction at his prosperity. From anger are produced strife, swelling of mind, insults, clamor, indignation, blasphemies."[2] These are the "capital"—that is, the "head" (Latin: *caput*)—sins, the cardinal sins, the sins that are among the most fecund of sins. Their seriousness is not so much within themselves but in their ability to generate even more serious offspring. Gregory the Great spoke of the Seven as "leaders of wicked armies."

Our local papers this week contain gruesome accounts of a man who, it is alleged, murdered his wife by stabbing her to death. Motive? A hundred-thousand-dollar life insurance policy. Greed is called deadly because of its children.

The church does not teach that these sins are "deadly," for they don't lead directly to damnation. They are more accurately called the *capital* or *cardinal* sins, the source, the "head," *the necessary first step toward other sin.* These sins were first known as "mortal" sins, a word that somehow sounds less lethal than "deadly." They are certainly endemic to humanity. "Human, all too human" are these sins. In fact, that's one thing that makes the Seven seem downright humorous to many in the world. They all seem so universally, ubiquitously human. Hitler's genocide is so much more significant and interesting than my inner thoughts about Nicole Kidman.

But the church meant *mortal* not in the sense of "typically human," but in the sense of leading one's soul to hell. These sins are more lethal to one's soul, more detrimental to one's relationship to God than the less significant "venial" sins. Venial sins are mere stumblings along the path of life, rather than a one-way trip to hellish separation from God.

And right here we discover the peculiar deadliness of the Seven. They are so ordinary, so pervasive in human life, all with their roots in basic, from-infancy human nature, that we may fail to see how terribly they warp our humanity. The lust of a couple of schoolboys, sneaking a look at the Playmate of the Month in *Playboy*, is fairly innocent stuff. And yet those same boys, surfing the web at forty, in the depths of pornography, betraying marriage vows for an exercise of lust, seems to me different altogether. Nearly all of the Seven look fairly harmless as they appear among adolescents but repulsive, ugly when exercised in middle age. Regarded thus they remind us that sin is not so much the popular "doing what you know you are not supposed to do" but rather a perverted *being who we are*. Which makes discussion of the Seven so very difficult because they are all so human. One might argue that bestiality is so inhuman as to be, well, *beastly*. But who would argue the same for envy or pride? As Solzhenitsyn said, "the line dividing good and evil cuts through the heart of every human being. And who is willing to destroy a piece of his own heart?"[3]

We are conceived in sin. We are rarely as unabashedly self-centered as we are in infancy—loudly demanding that our every need be met without regard for anyone else—and yet such self-centeredness is an essential requirement for the infant's survival. There is irony in noting that the perfectly understandable, necessary aspect of human life that preserves us in infancy brings us to such grief at forty. Our mortality is not only in that we will die, but that we live our lives in that creaturely insecurity whereby we attempt to secure our lives through the wrong means. We so want to establish ourselves through some means other than through life with our Creator on the Creator's terms. The larger sin of idolatry, setting up something else in our lives where God ought to be, is progenitor of the Seven.

One justification for calling the Seven "deadly" is that they are difficult to shake; chronic. I haven't agonized much over whether or not to commit murder; even the thought of adultery has been far from my mind. Really spectacular sins like genocide are out of my reach. Yet the seemingly minor and so much more democratic, plebian sins of envy and anger seem more tempting with my passage into late middle age. Many of the young people to whom I minister think that we get better as we get older. True, lust seems to require more conscious effort after sixty than at sixteen. Yet the inclination of the old to feel despair over the lack of life's accomplishments suggests that with the accumulation of

8

years comes the tendency to the sins that breed in the fertile soil of regret—sloth, envy, anger, to mention but three.

Some sins do appear to weaken their hold over our imaginations with the passage of years. A youthful inclination toward patricide or matricide lessens as we get older and our parents pace peacefully into the past, having already done us any harm many years ago. Freud, Marx, and other makers of modernity appear to have had as their major project the techniques for ridding us of our parents. Who needs Freud after you are sixty and who wants Marx hanging around after your house is paid for? Inclination toward adultery eventually becomes a simple matter of inevitable decline in libido. But the ravages of time and the decline of physical prowess do nothing to lessen the power of the Seven over our lives; in fact, it seems to increase. I write these words, trudging toward sixty, bearing on my back an assortment of the Seven as robust as ever.

Evagrius was clear that it is quite human to have these sins in our *thoughts*. The deadliness is when we yield to them. He says, "It is not in our power to determine within us or not, and whether or not they are to stir up our passions." Which helps explain why *acedia*, sloth, is for him one of the most serious of the Seven.

Today we are encouraged to "stir up our passions," and passion, desire, can certainly be a good thing. The dean of our divinity school, when asked what was the one characteristic he would like to see in divinity students, said "passion." Contra Evagrius, I think, would argue that our sin stems not from a surfeit of desire but rather from a paucity of desire for the right things. Envy may be a result of too much passionate ambition, but envy is sometimes the punishment for a life too slothfully lived.

I don't know why there are seven deadly sins and not four or twenty. Before Gregory there were eight, specifically related to the demands of monastic life. Galatians 5:19-21 lists sins, but the Bible is not the source of the traditional lists of vices. Medieval list makers struggled to find support in the Bible for their lists, but it is the nature of these sins that they appear to have rather shaky scriptural foundation. One of my challenges, in this book, will be to read the Seven theologically and biblically, attempting to give a specifically Christian account of the Seven.

Gregory groped to discover some scriptural basis for this particular Seven. He was fond of heptads of opposition, suggesting, for example, that the Seven Sins somehow related to the seven petitions of the Lord's Prayer. In Luke 8:2 Jesus exorcises seven devils from Mary Magdalene, thus giving Gregory the Great about the only biblical support he could muster for the seven-sin scheme. The number seven makes its appearance briefly in Proverbs 6:16-19: "These things the Lord hates..." Seven is the number of days in the week, and there are Seven Last Words of Christ, Seven Gifts of the Spirit in Isaiah 11, Seven Hills of Rome, and Seven Brides for Seven Brothers. *Hebdomania.* Make of all this what you will.

One would think there might be ten, related to the Ten Commandments. But the Seven are rather curiously, or notoriously, disconnected from the concerns of the Ten Commandments, though as we shall later note, Envy is certainly a close cousin of the "covetousness" condemned there. Few have been interested in expanding the list of the Seven Deadly Sins—we have enough trouble with the sins we've got without finding more. Protestant Reformers largely rejected and ridiculed the Seven because there is lack of biblical warrant.

More typical, particularly in the modern era, have been reductionistic attempts to subsume all of the Seven into one. In a college religion course, I was told that when the Bible says *sin* it is basically talking about pride. Around a first-class, selective university that accredits the upwardly mobile for a lifetime of success, there are days when I think greed covers just about everything. Yet there is much to be said for letting the sins stay at seven, thus indicating the richness and the diversity of our perversity.

In medieval art, the Seven Deadly Sins are often portrayed as personalities. They are embodied, usually as ugly and disgusting people. Gluttony, for instance, is always a fat man with porcine features, swilling and drinking, head down in trough, rear end flatulating. Envy is a wasted, sickly woman.

This sort of ugly personification seems unfortunate because part of the fascination of the Seven is that they can all be so seductively attractive. When gluttony dresses up and indulges in a six-course meal in a nice restaurant, and the cost of the meal is considered as much as the quantity consumed, then it is a fit subject for praise on the Food Channel, rather than condemnation in a sermon. Many call my much-lamented "pride" merely healthy-minded "self-esteem." There is a fine line between that Sabbath rest that is the grace of doing nothing, the sort of languor of youth that characterizes the masses in the Duke Gardens on a Saturday afternoon, and the slothful inability to get out of bed and worship God on a Sunday morning. Anger can be red-blooded, prophetic, righteous indignation against injustice or white-hot prelude to violence. We thank God that Martin Luther King had the moral sensitivity to get mad at racial injustice. The line between virtue and vice is subtle, and its subtlety is an aspect of its deadliness.

In his "Marriage of Heaven and Hell," William Blake notes that pride in the peacock is glorious, lust in the goat is endearing, and so many of those things that we call "vice" can be, in the right context, in the right person, "virtue." Aquinas attempts to honor this subtlety when he, following his mentor Aristotle, presents our vices as virtue in excess. *Virtue* comes from the Latin word *virtus*, which means "manliness" (from *vir*), that which makes us human. We still say "by virtue of" or speak of "virtuosity." *Vice* comes from *vitium*, meaning "deficiency," "lack."

I have never liked that sense in which our word *sin* comes from the Hebrew and Greek, meaning "missing the mark." Our sins seem considerably more significant than a mere mess up, a minor missing of the mark. And yet when it comes to the Seven, that is a good way to think of them. Missing the mark. We set out to live the abundant life, to achieve more. And we end up by merely hoarding a mess of inconsequential possessions. We want to connect with another person, to find romance and love, and it slips into mere lust. In talking about the Seven Deadly Sins, we are talking about those virtues that make us most human, to be as we are most created to be. Sometimes it does seem as if our vices are the other side of goodness, virtue having gotten out of hand. Nothing in excess. Moderation in all things. The Golden Mean.

We call an act courageous, says Aristotle, because it has managed to steer a moderate course between recklessness and cowardice.

But in my reckoning, this sort of moderated, Aristotelian thinking is not that helpful in dealing with the Seven. Envy is both too insidious and too complex to be cured through moderation. Moreover, all appeals to Aristotelian moderation seem incongruent with the thought of Jesus. Can you imagine Jesus saying, "A little lust, in the service of the noble pursuit of love, can be a good thing"? When something so minor as "lust in the eye" led Jesus to call for radical surgery, this is not moderation. Gluttony is certainly something more than the love of good that has forgotten its manners.

Aristotle spoke of "the unity of the virtues," the notion that virtues tend to cluster around one another. If a person has one virtue, such as temperance, then one is not surprised to find some of the other virtues residing in her as well. While Aristotle did not, I would extend this observation about the virtues to vices as well. Show me that person who has given in to greed, and I would not be surprised to find him an enthusiastic practitioner of lust and gluttony as well. I don't think I have ever known envy to not also be strolling, hand-in-hand, with anger, though I can't recall having ever seen sloth and lust as bedfellows. Excuse the pun.

Virtues, for all their virtue, do not balance the weight of vices. Vices tend to predominate over some of even the most noble virtues, in the same way as a recessive gene dominates when mixed with other genetic combinations. A novel about a person who was unfailingly courageous, chaste, and generous would be a boring piece of fiction. Milton failed, in his *Paradise Lost*, to make

Satan less interesting than Christ. Working together, in various combinations, the Seven are a potent force. Courage, blended with lust, is a frightening mix. Good Lord deliver us from those insufferably righteous folk who (often hanging out around churches and college faculties) manage to mix anger with envy and appeals to some abstract ideal like "peace with justice."

Saint Thomas Aquinas contended that the really sinful thing about sin is in the committing of the act, the doing of the sin. He knew that the Christian notion of Original Sin makes us thoroughly sinful beings rather than simply those incipiently good people who from time to time commit sinful acts. Aquinas notes that thoughts lead to acts and that intentions are the prelude to action, so that, when you think about it, thinking is doing. Aquinas was attempting to stress that there is a big difference between thinking evil and actually doing it. Luther said much the same with his famous comment about our not being able to keep the birds from flitting around our heads, but having a duty to keep them from nesting in our hair. Who on earth would criticize us for merely *thinking* murderous thoughts, while successfully restraining ourselves from committing murder?

Jesus, that's who. The only time he outright said that somebody could send himself to hell, it was for speaking ill of one's neighbor. Jesus took away from his followers the perfectly natural, completely understandable, universal inclination to name our neighbor "thou fool!" (Edmund Burke said, in 1796, "All men that are ruined are ruined on the side of their natural propensities.") Why would Jesus not confine himself only to lustful action, rather than condemn the relatively harmless "lust of the heart"?

14

Here we come closer to an understanding of what makes sin, sin for Christians. For those of us who are trying to take Jesus seriously, sin is not a foible, a slipup; it is offense against and rebellion against our Creator. Sin is that which separates us from a holy and righteous God. Jesus makes the rather astounding claim that, when it comes to sin, it's the thought that counts. Sin not only hurts the neighbor who is sinned against but also reflexively bites the sinner too. Sin carries within itself its own punishment. It erodes the soul. It severs an intended relationship between Creator and creature. These sins are called sins because of the nature of God in Jesus Christ, not from some view of human nature. But more about that later.

Aristotle, whom Aquinas followed more closely than Scripture in thinking about why the Seven Sins are sins, notes that people never see evil as evil. People are created, or conditioned, thought Aristotle, always to seek what is apprehended as good, that which adds to the joy of life, and to avoid what they believe to be evil. Therefore if someone pursues some harmful course of action, it is because of a failure to perceive it as wrong. Aristotle, like Plato before him, had great faith that if we know what is good for us we will quite logically pursue it. Our "sin" is mostly a matter of a failure to know what is good for us, a failure of the intellect rather than of willpower.

Christian theology, particularly the theology of the Reformation, has generally taken a much more robust assessment of our sin. Our sinful nature is so deeply rooted in all our thought and action that no amount of clear thinking and clench-fisted determination can overcome it. Paul wrote that he could know the good but he could not do the good.

In fact, the story of Jesus nailed to the cross teaches Christians that our virtues are not merely the opposite of our vices but sometimes the royal road to the worst of our evil. Jesus was crucified for the very best of human good reasons such as peace, justice, doctrinal fidelity, national security, and on and on. We are rarely more murderous than when we are defending some noble ideal like freedom or democracy.

From the face of it, I can't figure out why Sloth makes the list. Name me one battle that has ever been fought, one murder committed, one marital dalliance pursued out of Sloth? Most of us enjoy being around "laid-back" people. For a sometimes compulsive, passionately productive person like me, it would be moral progress for me to put an "I'd rather be at the beach" bumper sticker on my car.

Care must be taken before dismissing any of the Seven. We live in a society in which just about every vice has been repackaged, humored, and presented as a virtue. Type A personalities have been urged to soak longer in the bath; Sloth can be good for your high blood pressure. What on earth, pray tell, would Madison Avenue advertising do without Envy as their major marketing device? While I would not go so far as to say that capitalism is built on Greed, it sure knows how to put Greed to good use.

In Augustine's *Confessions*, Book II, in the infamous episode about the stealing of the pears, Augustine magnifies a sin that seems so inconsequential. By this time in the account of his life, Augustine has fathered a child out of wedlock, has hinted at many youthful indiscretions. And yet when he comes to the prime example of his deep perversity, he gives as evidence the stealing of a few pears. Is Augustine being overscrupulous?

Augustine was notoriously convinced of his own great sinfulness. He presents adolescence as a time when "I cared for nothing but to love and be loved" (2.2). The theft of pears by a group of boys may not seem to us like a great sin, but it becomes for Augustine a revelation of the way in which his problem is not simply the sins that he commits, but his inclination toward sin. He finds that the human being is fascinated with some actions simply because the actions are illicit and prohibited.

He and some friends steal a few pears from a neighbor's pear tree, not because they are hungry or need to steal the pears, but from *eo liberet quo non liceret,* "that which is not permitted allured us," which is to say, just for the hell of it. The important thing is not the transgression, for perhaps Augustine intends for the transgression to be pointedly of minor moral significance. Rather the problem is the inclination, the desire.

In the Christian faith, an act or inclination, a passion or an emotion is sinful to the degree that it alienates us from God by offending God. Sin is about God. To those who do not know, or do not serve this God, the Seven are bound to seem rather silly, much ado about nothing. Thus we are not to seek the seriousness and significance of the Seven by uncovering their deleterious effects upon human life, but rather the way in which each, in its own way, and in concert, violates the nature of God. Because it is of the nature of God in Christ to offer selfless, self-emptying love (Philippians 2), Lust is a sin. Because the Son of God is the one who stoops and serves, Pride is a sin. Because God is the source of all that we have and all that we are, to envy someone else is to make Envy more than an unattractive personality characteristic; Envy is sin. Because Jesus taught us to pray for no more than "our daily bread," lust for more bread, Gluttony, is a sin.

But the very first thing that we are to do with sin is not to point to it in others but rather to confess it in ourselves. "Remember that you are dust and to dust you shall return," the church's admonition to us on Ash Wednesday, is another way of saying, "Remember that you are a sinner."

While sin is not the defining aspect of a human being, nor is it the chief concern of our life with God, our life with God enables us openly to confess our sin and to begin again, to get up, to go on, to resume our journey with God.

God does not command us to do impossible things. With God's grace, we can be more than conquerors through him who loves us. The main reason to spend all this effort talking about sin is so that we can name it, claim it, and move on to more significant lives than if we had lied about ourselves. We investigate sin, stare it in the face, admit its reality and its ravages, so that we may be on our way to fulfillment of God's great promise to God's people, "You shall be holy, for I the LORD your God am holy" (Leviticus 19:2). All of God's sweeping commands and all of Jesus' high expectations are meant to be heard by us as vocation, that abundant life that we are meant to live. Righteousness, freedom from the Seven, virtuous life, is meant to be not some impossible ideal, but rather a gift that is offered:

> Surely, this commandment that I am commanding you today is not too hard for you, nor is it too far away. It is not in heaven.... Neither is it beyond the sea.... No, the word is very near to you; it is in your mouth and in your heart for you to observe. (Deuteronomy 30:11-14)

CHAPTER TWO

PRIDE

If Pride be a sin, it is a specifically Christian sin. Not simply because Christians routinely are guilty of Pride, but also because we would not know that Pride is a sin were it not for the example of Jesus. When Karl Barth said that only Christians really sin, surely he had the sin of Pride in mind. That is, if one were not attempting to listen to and follow Jesus, I can't imagine why one would know that Pride is a bad thing.

Pride, considered in itself, can be a most attractive virtue. We parents try to instill a sense of "self-worth" (Pride) in our children. The other day a man showed me a beautiful coffee table that he had made out of a single piece of oak. "I'm proud of that one," he said. "My hands made that." I was charmed.

To be sure, too much Pride is called "arrogance," but the beneficial effects of Pride—a sense of achievement, a desire for excellence, an aspiration to do the best that you can do—all outweigh any deleterious by-products of hubris.

Pride is rather remarkable in that none of the other Seven, in any fashion, have enjoyed the benevolent transformation that Pride has undergone in recent years. It is not an overstatement to say that Pride has moved from being the chief of the Seven, the root of much evil, to being the root of all virtue, a positive good to be lovingly practiced and cultivated. Pride has been rehabilitated from being a vice to be avoided and has become a great virtue to be cultivated—Black Pride, Gay Pride, Southern Pride, and on and on.

I recently heard a management guru declare, "There is no more important quality to cultivate among the workers in a company than pride in their products." Our political life seems dominated now by the politics of self-assertion, and our therapies are mostly the relentless psychology of vaunted self-esteem. The great sin for us is not Pride, but low self-image. Somehow Pride and its cousins—arrogance, egotism, vanity, and conceit—got trumped by self-respect, self-esteem, self-confidence, and self-ascribed dignity. Jesus' exhortation to "love thy neighbor as thyself" has been shortened to a hard and fast, ruthlessly enforced mandate: *love thyself!*

Perhaps, if we all were full of Pride and genuine self-esteem, then we would never know envy and there would never be conflict among us. The notoriously atheistic philosopher Bertrand Russell said, "I do not believe that any peacock envies another peacock his tail, because every peacock is persuaded that his own tail is the finest in the world. The consequence of this is that peacocks are peaceable birds."[1]

Philosopher Adam Smith joined Shaftesbury in attacking the old virtue/vice distinction of the Church Fathers, particularly in the Fathers' low estimate of Pride. Smith thought it unreasonable for the Fathers to condemn a healthy human drive like Pride. What the Fathers condemned as Pride is in reality that enlightened self-interest and creativity that can be the engine that drives society toward human betterment, said Smith and Shaftesbury. Take away Pride and you have a society of lethargic, slovenly creatures who are content to live in the mud. Pride is good. Greed is good. Encourage it, channel it if you must, harness it if you will, said Smith. Thus was the world that produced Donald Trump.

Pride is a rueful admission that who we think we are is often a function of who others believe us to be. Pride and shame tend to be heavily dependent on what others think about us. We attend colleges and join clubs, fraternities, gangs. I remember a time when college students had to wear fraternity Greek letters on their chests in order to pump up their self-esteem through their membership in the group. Now, they just wear the logos of "The Gap" or "Old Navy." My own personage may be small and weak, but in the group, together shouting "We're Number One!" I am somebody. Our self-worth can be considerably buoyed by a perception of the values of the group. David Hume thought of Pride as that pleasure engendered in us in our moments of self-approval. But even our moments of self-approval are often tethered to our expectation of the approval of others in what we do. Others become the mirror that we periodically gaze in and ask, "How am I doing?"

I am not so sure that low self-esteem is our greatest problem. Did the Nazis build on low German self-esteem in order to get power in Germany or just the opposite, building upon German delusions of national exceptionalism and Pride? I recall a conversation with a crusty old prison chaplain. I said something about all the people who were in jail because they suffered from a "warped sense of themselves," and he quickly corrected me. "That's horseshit. Those guys are not in jail because they think too little of themselves, but because they think too much of themselves. Every one of them thinks he's a brilliant mind who is above the poor saps who obey the rules, go to work, follow the law. Every one of them thinks he's a damn genius and his victims are stupid."

Dr. Harold Shipman was jailed for life in January of 2000 for murdering fifteen patients while working in Hyde, England. Police believed that he killed somewhere between 215 and 260 of his patients, making him the greatest serial killer in English history. On January 13, 2004, he was found hanging in his prison cell. Never once did Shipman show any remorse for his crimes. At his death, a lawyer for Shipman said, "He was the most arrogant, pride-filled man I ever met. I think he just killed all those people because he thought he was smart enough to do it."

Yet really now, is Pride so serious as to be considered a sin? There are those who have thought of Pride as more of an error of judgment, the mistake we make in judging ourselves in far too positive a way, than as a sin. As Spinoza put it, "Pride is thinking more highly of oneself than is just, out of love for oneself" (*Ethics* III). Spinoza then claimed that "no one ... thinks less highly of themselves than is just"—just the opposite of most self-help psychologists, who insist that self-love is the precondition of a happy life. When we take too much credit for our lives and our achievements, when we come to look at our lives as products of our own striving rather than gifts, we are moving close to that idolatry in which the creature refuses to give due to the Creator.

Aristotle praised the man who had "greatness of soul" (Pride) as opposed to the one who was foolishly vain or unduly humble (*Nicomachean Ethics*, 1123B, 1125A). Aristotle praised this sort of self-sufficient, magnanimous man who disdains praise and does not seek it but often gives it to others. And yet this can be just the sort of self-sufficiency that is condemned by Christians.

Arrogance and conceit are two of the sins that are fathered (or mothered) by the sin of Pride. Self-respect is one thing; self-infatuation is another. In noting that Pride is the first of the deadly sins, the root, we are reminded that these are the sins of the monastery, the sins that make life together difficult. My Pride usually poses no real problem to you, as long as we remain strangers. But if we should attempt to get together, to work on something in common, then Pride is a problem.

For one thing, Pride can lead me to spectacularly bad judgments. The person who thinks of himself as a genius is on his way to some really stupid mistakes. The warrior who thinks of himself as invincible isn't a warrior for long. An economist gave me a fascinating book, called *The Winner's Curse*[2] (why did he think I needed to read this book?). Author Richard Thaler, a renowned economist, notes that some of our greatest successes are a prelude to some of our worst failures. He studied gamblers in Las Vegas and found that their greatest losses usually followed their biggest wins. The gambler got on a winning streak, thought that he was lucky, that he was a genius at gambling, so he bet a huge stake and lost it all. The businessperson who has a string of business successes begins to think that he is a genius at finance, that the prosaic principles of good business practice don't apply to him. Then comes the downfall. This is "the winner's curse," the way that the biggest "winners" often end up as the biggest "losers." Although Thaler doesn't, I would call the "winner's curse" a result of Pride. "Pride goes before destruction, and a haughty spirit before a fall" (Proverbs 16:18).

Yet, to tell the truth, I can't think of much that is wrong with a healthy—within limits—sense of Pride *except that Jesus was against it.* Only a faith that believes that Jesus was the full revelation of God would consider Pride a sin. Jesus began his earthly work in a desert. The heavenly voice at his baptism proclaimed, "You are my Son, the Beloved…" (Luke 3:22). Yet though he was chock "full of the Holy Spirit" (4:1-2), that same Spirit led him into a wilderness where for "forty days he was tempted by the devil."

I tend to think of temptation as a midlife-crisis sort of thing, something that hits you on a late afternoon in middle age. But the gospel here portrays encounters with the devil as happening early in one's career; at least it was that way for Jesus.

In the desert there are no clear paths, so you have to make your own way. Without city walls and civil protection, you are on your own in the desert. This is one reason why most of us fear being alone for too long, and why we must always have music pumping into our ears. Alone, in the quiet, in the desert, voices come, and for Jesus, the voice that comes, after the heavenly baptismal voice, is that of the devil.

"If you are the Son of God," (that is, if you are who the heavenly voice said you were at your baptism), "command this stone to become a loaf of bread" (4:3). The person who could turn stones to bread could do a lot of good for poor, suffering humanity and would be canonized quicker than Mother Teresa. Jesus says, "No."

True, says Satan, feed a man today; he'll only be hungry again tomorrow. Then, if you are the Son of God, do some good for the greatest number through the only long-term, effective means of doing good that we know—politics. Then Satan, in an instant, shows Jesus "all the kingdoms of the world" (4:5) and offers to hand them and all "their glory and all this authority" (4:6) to Jesus, "for it has been given over to me, and I give it to anyone I please," if Jesus will just worship the devil.

(Here we pause to wonder, who gave the devil all the nations of the world? Did God say, "Politics? I have no interest in such grubby affairs. Here, Satan, I'll let you have politics"? We don't know. All we know is that, when it comes to politics, there does seem to be an obvious linkage with worship of the devil.)

At any rate, Jesus again refuses. He even refuses religious, spiritual feats (4:9-11), refusing to throw himself down from the top of the temple and ask for angelic help, even though the baptismal voice said that he was the Son of God.

Note that the temptations of the devil are not just any old temptations. This is not about the piece of chocolate pie after dinner or the tempting sweet young thing in the negligee. This is a peculiar, specific temptation, vocational temptation. It's a debate between the devil and Jesus over who Jesus is. Each of the temptations is preceded by the devil's "If you are . . . then. . . ." The baptismal voice has said, "This is my Son." If Jesus is indeed the very Son of God, so intimately connected with God, then he ought to act like God, or at least act like God would act if we were God—omnipotently. What is God if not unlimited, free, absolute power? And what is Pride but an exercise of, and a relishing in, our potency? This is what the serpent offered us, in offering us unlimited, unrestrained wisdom back in the Garden: "Your eyes will be opened, and you will be like God" (Genesis 3:5). Thus was the modern university founded.

And yet, Jesus says no.

Luke says that Satan sulked away, leaving Jesus "until an opportune time" (Luke 4:13). We hear no more of the devil or his temptations until the end of the Jesus story. As Jesus hangs on the cross in mortal agony, the devil's words are repeated nearly verbatim. The soldiers, those in the employ of the "kingdoms of this world," mock Jesus, saying, "If you are the King of the Jews, save yourself" (Luke 23:37). And the crowd (that's us) screams, "Are you not the Messiah? Save yourself and us!" (23:39). Satan doesn't have to tempt Jesus this time. Now the devil's words are on our lips.

If you are the Son of God, then act like it! Act like our definition of God. Don't be who God says you are; be who we say you are! Jesus does not quote Scripture this time, as he did in the wilderness. He just hangs there in humiliation and defeat, in weakness and in shame. He says no to the devil with his silence. The last temptation of Christ takes place as he hangs on the cross, his last temptation to be the God we thought we deserved.

Jesus encounters the temptation to Pride with his rejection and with his silence. Has this God, and this Son of God, no Pride?

What is more, early Christian writers saw Jesus' pattern on the cross not only as his nature but as our vocation as well. Paul writes to the Philippians:

> Let the same mind be in you that was in Christ Jesus,
> who, though he was in the form of God,
>   did not regard equality with God
>   as something to be exploited,
> but emptied himself,
>   taking the form of a slave,
>   being born in human likeness.
> And being found in human form,
>   he humbled himself
>   and became obedient to the point of death—
>   even death on a cross. (Philippians 2:5-8)

It is a shock to see, revealed in Jesus, "the form of God." This is not at all what we expected of God or God's Messiah. Furthermore, if this self-emptying, humble servanthood is the shape of God, how is it possible for us frail, vulnerable, threatened, and therefore so very self-seeking creatures to have the "same mind that was in Christ Jesus"?

Aquinas says that Pride is the first sin of the Seven, the chief sin, the opposite of the virtue of Charity. He cites but one verse, the apocryphal Ecclesiasticus 10:15, for support: "Pride is the beginning of all sin" (*Summa Theologica* I, 2, Q.84. art.2). Yet we

find in Aquinas a certain reluctance to call Pride the most griev-
ous of sins because Pride, of all the Seven, is the most difficult to
avoid. "What is more difficult to guard against than Pride?"
Thomas asks. Furthermore he recalls that Augustine said that
Pride, unlike some sins, is not just in the act but also in the dis-
position, lying "in wait even for good deeds to destroy them."
Pride is first something that you feel before it is anything you do.
Thus Pride can transform even the most noble virtues into a sin.
George Bernard Shaw says he detests hell as "the home of honor,
duty, justice, and the rest of the seven deadly virtues" (*Man and
Superman*, 3). Besides, says Thomas, anyone can see that Lust is
a sin (at least, anyone could see the sin of Lust back then), yet
Pride is more subtle, tainting even our deeds of "justice and
virtue." Thomas even says that sometimes God allows us to succumb to other, less grave sins than Pride, just to remedy our tendency toward Pride. The penitent sinner who knows that he has
sinned in Lust, Sloth, or Gluttony is, as it were, innoculated
against the greater, more dangerous sin of Pride.

Dante, in *Purgatorio* 9-28, organizes sins in a fashion that was
perfected in medieval times. In canto 17, Virgil explains to Dante
about the sins. Sin, says Virgil, is misdirected love. Surely Pride is
the prime example of sin as misdirected love. Love can be
directed toward an evil object—as in Pride, Envy, and Wrath—
or toward a good object like rest, as in Sloth (where love of rest
is defective) or in Gluttony (where love of food is excessive). The
Seven, said the medieval theologians, are radical distortions of
love. If that is true, then Pride is otherwise admirable self-love
(Jesus commands us to love our neighbor as much as we love

ourselves) gotten out of hand, love that ought to be given only to God, given to the self as if the self were God. In his *Parson's Tale*, Chaucer refers to the Seven at length, comparing the sins to a tree whose branches produce twigs that go in many different directions. At the root is Pride.

I like this idea of Pride as misdirected love, as love perverted and misapplied. This points to the insidious, subtle quality of much of our sin. If sin were a matter of performing some self-evident, obvious wrong, then we would never be sinners. Yet sin is rarely self-evidently bad. It takes training, analysis, and much living and reflection, prayer, and quiet consideration to be a sinner. One must be taught to sin—that is, to know sin when one does it. The rest of the world, uninformed by the story of Jesus, considers Pride an essential characteristic of the well-functioning personality. Christians are taught to be more suspicious.

Although we may question whether or not Pride is the root of all sin, or the greatest of sins, it does appear in the Scriptures as one of the oldest. As we have noted, the serpent appealed to the Pride of Adam and Eve. It was the Pride of Cain that led him so to resent Abel that he killed him (Genesis 4:1-26). Pride built Babel's tower (Genesis 11). The serpent's promise, "You will be like God...," is repeated, in so many words, in our ambitious building project at Babel: "Come, let us build ourselves a city, and a tower with its top in the heavens, and let us make a name for ourselves" (Genesis 11:4). Without Pride, we would have no great cities, no United Nations, no international cooperation, no great symphonies, or any other of our collective attempts to "make a name for ourselves."

Still, Christians are conditioned to name human self-assertion as a subspecies of the sin of idolatry, setting ourselves up as gods. What the world calls healthy "self-esteem," Christians sniff out as idolatry, self-worship. The devil in the desert had it right in telling Jesus that he could be empowered to set the world right, to correct all of God's mistakes at creation; all that was necessary was to "worship me" and "all this will be yours."

A member of our faculty recently justified to me his disbelief of Christianity by saying that "with all the suffering and pain in the world, I just can't see how you can call God good. I am very sensitive to the plight of others."

I'm sure that he thinks of himself as a humble, sincere disbeliever. Another way of looking at him is that he considers himself better, more sensitive, and more caring than the God who would make such a lousy world. If *he*—with his master's degree and his global sensitivity—had been God, he would have made a better world. It's the serpent's promise, "You will be like gods. . . ."

I've got a Jewish friend who is fond of saying, "Jews have two major beliefs: (1) there is a God; (2) you are not it."

As Aquinas noted, Pride is a virtually unavoidable sin. Tell someone, "Jesus wants you to be good, to do the right thing, to work for justice," and Pride says, "I'll take over from here." What does God want out of us? Only that we "do justice, and to love kindness, and to walk humbly with your God" (Micah 6:8). As tough as it is to do justice and to adore kindness, when Micah adds that we should "walk humbly with your God," if we have an ounce's worth of self-knowledge we are apt to throw up our hands. How is it possible to achieve even a modicum of justice and kindness in this life and also be humble about it?

"Good is the enemy of great. And that is one of the key reasons why we have so little that becomes great." Thus begins Jim Collins's management book, *Good to Great*. Collins tells how eleven great companies overcame the mediocrity of being merely good and dared creatively to launch out and be great.

Yet Collins could as well have said that the Christian faith, with its stress upon goodness, particularly humble goodness, is the archenemy of great. It is not only that Christians are called to be good rather than great, called to be saints rather than heroes, but also there is built into the faith a deep suspicion of those who would be great. When my friend Stanley Hauerwas was named "The Best Theologian in America" by *Time*, Hauerwas thanked them for the honor and then told them that, as Christians, we don't consider "best" to be one of our categories. Jesus leans decidedly toward the "wretched of the earth" and has some choice, severe words for the high and the mighty, the best and the brightest.

Paul urges us, in Philippians, to renounce "selfish ambition." Perhaps the stress ought to be upon the adjective. It's the "selfish" ambition that's of the wrong sort. Yet in the same letter Paul continually exhorts the faithful to think about and to embody all that is good, to have within us the very "mind of Christ." That sounds ambitious, spiritually speaking, and even if I earnestly desire self-improvement, that little qualifier "self" so quickly transmogrifies into "selfish." Paradoxically, it is that "mind of Christ" who "emptied himself, taking the form of a servant," that mind who so severely judges our ambition, even our ambition to be good, and makes it look selfish.

J. D. Salinger, in talking about those "honest" writers who use their literature to confess their sins, said, "A confessional passage has probably never been written that didn't stink a little bit of the writer's pride in having given up his pride."[3] Pride insinuates itself even into our praise of humility. Some years ago the late David H. C. Read, a Presbyterian pastor in New York, suggested that, though hypocrisy and self-righteousness are typically ecclesiastical sins, today's real hypocrites may not be those who, like the proud Pharisee, pray, "God, I'm thankful I'm not like those sinners outside the church," but rather those who say, with more than a little Pride, "I may not be the best person in the world but at least I am better than those hypocritical Christians in the church." Though Pride may breed freely among those who would be good, even those who would be good have no corner on this sin. "I have often wished I had time to cultivate modesty," said Dame Edith Sitwell in a 1950 interview, "but I am too busy thinking about myself."

Two old men sitting in their synagogue during the Sabbath service overhear the loud lament of another worshiper near them: "God, be merciful to me, a nobody! God, forgive me, a nobody! God, help me, though I'm a nobody!"

One of the men looks at the other and asks, "Who's this who thinks he's such a nobody?"

Even in our honest confession of our sin, there can be the whiff of Pride.

Addressing those "who trusted in themselves that they were righteous and regarded others with contempt," Jesus told a story of two men who went to the Temple to pray (Luke 18:9-14). One, a sleazy, good-for-nothing tax collector collaborator with the Romans and swindler of his own people, prayed, "God, be merciful to me, a sinner." He had nothing, claimed nothing, and sought everything. He wasn't acting humble; he was publicly humiliated.

The other man, an outstanding, righteous, sacrificial, Bible-obeying person, prayed, "God, I thank you that I am not like other people: thieves, rogues, adulterers, or even like this tax-collector. I fast twice a week; I give a tenth of all my income." He is not only a good man, but also a really good man who does what Jesus urged and goes the second mile in his living and his giving. His virtues he regards as gifts ("God, I thank you that...") rather than as his achievements.

Still, Jesus lands a zinger in saying, "I tell you, this man [the cheating scoundrel] went down to his home justified rather than the other; for all who exalt themselves will be humbled, but all who humble themselves will be exalted."

What on earth are we supposed to do with that? "OK, gang, let's get out there and really be humble this week. Let's see if we can out-humble the Baptists." The tax collector's humility wasn't a virtue, something he had worked at. It was simply a realistic assessment of his situation. He was a failure at being righteous. He had no hope of setting things right between himself and God, except God.

Perhaps the Fathers of the Church called Pride the chief sin, the very first sin, in an admirably honest attempt to address that particular sin of "good" people first, the sin one most likely would find hanging out at the church, the sin most likely to breed among faithful, good people—such as people who might read a book on the Seven Deadly Sins. I'm proud that the Fathers put Pride first. Downright humble of them. C. S. Lewis called Pride "the great sin" and devoted an entire chapter of *Mere Christianity* to Pride alone.

We are what we worship. Aquinas noted that Pride is a turning-away from God. It is worship wrongly ordered. It is the sin of Faust, the sin that is the refusal to stay in one's proper place, the sin of the upwardly mobile. It is thinking of oneself as the Creator rather than the creature. In fact, without a belief in God, I can't figure out why Pride ought to be condemned. Perhaps that is why Pride has become a virtue, with the pushing of God out of the world. Pride is essentially a liturgical matter, a matter of wrong worship. Whereas most of the other sins really need no theological justification, when it comes to Pride, without the theology, I can't figure out much justification for considering it a sin. Pride may make people annoying, difficult to live with, in need of some good-natured deflation, but it is not a "sin"—*unless Jesus says so.*

Christians are trained to agree with the Jewish mystic philosopher Martin Buber when he says, "The struggle with evil must begin within one's own soul."[4] My sin is the problem, not yours; my Pride, not yours. If you are not attempting to be a Christian, I can't imagine why you would be troubled by your sense of Pride. If there is no God, then Pride can be a healthy, creative response to the emptiness of the world.

But for those of us who are following the way of Christ, stumbling along after him, to be sure, but still following, then our

Pride—our subtle, deceitful, intra-ecclesial Pride—is the first sin that we must consider and confess. Our Pride is part of our self-deceit, our lying about our real situation. As frail, mortal, vulnerable creatures, we react to our vulnerability in futile ways, one of them being our Pride. There is something incredibly pitiful about modern, twenty-first–century North American people telling ourselves that our greatest need is for more self-esteem, more self-confidence, more self-assurance—pitifully revealing how little esteem, confidence, or assurance that we have in ourselves. Or course, from a Christian point of view, that's the problem—ourselves.

Although I don't know if the point of the story is about the sin of Pride, Jesus told a story (Luke 12:16-21) about a rich farmer who said to himself, "What should *I* do, for *I* have no place to store *my* crops?" . . . "*I* will do this: *I* will pull down *my* barns and build large ones, . . . *I* will store all *my* grain and *my* goods. . . . *I* will say to *my* soul, . . ." (emphasis added). Note the extensive use of the first-person pronoun in this man's soliloquy. For those who are self-confident, self-sufficient, most of their talk is in monologue rather than dialogue. Here is a competent, able, prudent businessperson who knows how to protect and handle his self-accrued abundance. As the undertaker drags him out feet first, God calls him "Thou fool." We are the builders of bridges, makers of cities, writers of books, gatherers of money, who also decay and die.

And we would not have had such a problem with ourselves, would not have had to worry so much about a matter like Pride, had we not been encountered by Jesus, the One who told us not only the truth about ourselves but also the truth about God. He told us that we were frail creatures who react to our immortality in inappropriate ways, who find ourselves gods of our own liking who promise to pump us up to appropriate size and durability. All of our strutting about, our preening and positioning, is only a kind of backhanded validation of the strong biblical truth that we are created as dust and to dust shall we return (Genesis 3:19).

The most moving moment in Sunday worship for me is when my people come forward, at Holy Communion, streaming down toward the altar, and there they hold out empty hands like little children, like the famished folk they really are, empty, needing a gift in the worst sort of way. I think that is one of the most difficult, countercultural gestures of Christian worship—outstretched empty hands. What's normal, and natural, is the clinched fist, the hands grabbing and holding tight to what they can get. What's strange, from the world's point of view, is the openhanded, needy, empty request for grace.

I submit to you that there is no way that people like us (we have our master's degrees!) could hold out our empty, seeking hands had not the church taught us to do so, had not the church inculcated this honest gesture among us. This is who we are, says Jesus, not big, self-sufficient adults, but rather little children, naked, frail, empty, and hungry, needing a gracious God in the worst sort of way. You can't get into this Kingdom if you are all grown up and big and important. You can only come in through a very small door as an inept, bumbling, ignorant, and empty little child.

But most of all, Jesus tells us the truth about God. God is more than omnipotent, omniscient, and all those other non-biblical attributes that we would like to ascribe to God. God is the lowest and the least, the little one, the wretched, the one who hangs in agony on a cross, the one who stoops down and washes our feet, the one who emptied himself in order to get down on our level, the one who rose and thereby shall raise us up as well.

If we would worship this God, if we would follow him down his narrow, Nazarene way rather than parade down the world's wide boulevards, there will be some stooping on our part, too.

And I don't like to stoop. Do you? I don't like to turn and become as a little child. I like to be in charge, in command, on top. In my more dishonest moments, I think I may be somebody who has done something, something approximating the immortal. Thus Pride is virtually unavoidable. I may keep my nose clean of Gluttony, Lust, and even Envy, on my better days. But Pride is me all over, good days and bad, a by-product of the world's acclaim when my life is doing well, a strategy for self-preservation when my life is not doing well. I might be able to present myself to you as a basically good person, were it not for Pride being the first of the Seven. I sin, and sometimes when I'm doing the best I can, that, thanks to Pride, is my worst sin.

Being in the church helps. Often the community is able to show and to tell us things that we cannot learn from anyone else, anywhere else. Fortunately I have a few Christian friends who love me enough, and love the truth enough, to puncture some of my Pride. The Holy Spirit works through the community as a remedy against some of our sin.

Still, I sin. Even in my attempts at rehabilitation, I sin. Fortunately, the Scriptures are unanimous: Jesus came to seek, and to save, only sinners.

The way I see it, the sin of Pride is unavoidable. I am, as Luther noted, both a sinner and a justified, forgiven sinner at the same time. Therefore we have reason to be grateful that Jesus comes to seek and to save only the lost (Luke 19:10), only sinners. The pride-filled ungodly (Romans 5:6). Thanks be to God.

CHAPTER THREE

ENVY

At the table, as Jesus went forth to die, the disciples asked, "Who will get to sit at your right hand when you enter your kingdom?" (Luke 22:24ff., paraphrased). Even after Jesus' rather laborious reiteration of the place of servanthood in his Kingdom, even as he kneels before us with basin and towel, washing our feet, even as he goes forth to suffer a humiliating death, we all still want to be Number One. And the usual way we make Number One is by slithering up on the backs of others.

Although we might want to regard Envy as a mere human foible, there is good reason to take it more seriously. For one thing, Envy is one of the few deadly sins that have a direct coun-terpart in the Ten Commandments, with a command against covetousness. (True, the Ten Commandments don't get around to Envy until next to the last.) Murder, adultery, and theft are things that we *do*; Envy is, like many of the other Seven, some-thing we *feel*. Some say that only covetous *deeds* are what the Ninth Commandment condemns, but I doubt that we can get off the hook that easily. The Bible generally does not know our mod-ern dichotomies of inner/outer, personal/social, and private/pub-lic. To think a deed is to do it, as Jesus says when he equates lustful thoughts with adulterous acts. Matters of the heart matter; our dispositions and inclinations are, at least to Jesus, as significant as our actions. Christians believe that God has created humanity with restless hearts, imbuing us with an insatiable desire that can only be satisfied and find rest in the arms of the God who created us.

Contrary to what some might think, Christians regard desire as a good, God-created attribute of our humanity. Alas, failing to alight on the true object who is the source of our deepest desire—God—we consume everything else that we can get our hands on. Eluding God's attempt to get God's hands on us, we grab for every other false god. Christianity is, in part, the sort of moral, mental hygiene that occurs when our desires are formed and reformed toward their proper object.

In our most vigorous account of the Seven in early English lit-erature, *Piers Plowman*, Envy is personified with a snakelike tongue. *Piers* placed Envy in London among the merchants, busi-ness people, which I find somewhat surprising since I have seen

Envy flourish most effusively in academia or among clergy. Envy is more than jealousy. Jealousy is, by my definition, more a crime of passion, a more active, resourceful sort of sin than Envy. Envy attempts to keep to itself, is shy to reveal its real feelings, seethes, and stews in resentment because of the good fortune of another. Some have found it surprising that "hate" is not listed among the Seven. Hate seems so much more robust and vigorous than Envy. Yet I love the fact that Envy, as a sort of refined, subtle form of hate, is numbered among the Seven. Envy is less obviously sinful than crude, publicly expressed hate, but it can be no less deadly.

Evagrius calls Envy "sadness," which I think gets Envy just about right. Aquinas (in his *Summa Theologica*, II, 2, Q.36) looks upon Envy as a sort of sorrow, saying, "the object both of charity and of Envy is our neighbor's good, but by contrary movements, since charity rejoices in our neighbor's good, while Envy grieves over it...." Aquinas says that Envy is that sin of wishing that things were other than they are with your life, which, when you think about it, is sad. In article 6, point 6 of his *Summa*, Aquinas says that "Envy is a special sort of sorrow over another's goods." Special sort of sorrow indeed.

Lust and anger have a warm-hearted, hot-blooded, "human-all-too-human" quality about them. Envy is cold-blooded and cruel, even among friends, especially there. Most of the other Seven can be fun, let's admit it. Lust is at least momentarily pleasurable; so is gluttony. But who enjoys Envy, even for a moment?

When we Envy someone, we tend to magnify that person's good fortune while at the same time minimizing our own. The sun seems to shine more brightly upon them than us. They appear to live a charmed life. We, on the other hand, must be the victims of lousy luck. In Envy, there is a kind of diminishment of ourselves, which is one of the things that makes this sin so sad. Miguel Unamuno, Spanish novelist and philosopher, when asked to explain the viciousness of his country's civil war, called Envy "the spiritual leprosy of Spain," that hateful "resentment of intelligence."

Though Envy resents the neighbor, paradoxically, in Envy we have one of the most social of sins, a kind of homage to the neighbor. Whereas Gluttony or apathy perform quite fine in solo, it takes at least two to Envy. If Christianity is indeed a social, communal religion, as I hold it to be, then we ought to expect Envy to thrive among the faithful.

Envy, invidious comparison, is a subtle matter, but quite powerful. It gnaws, nibbles away at our consciousness. Paul says, in 1 Corinthians 13, that "love rejoices in the right." But it is sometimes a very difficult thing when right comes the way of even our very best friends. So H. L. Mencken said that, in America, contentment is making $10 a month more than your brother-in-law.[1]

When Jesus told us to "love your enemies," or even to "love your neighbor," his teaching was nowhere more against our inclination. Envy makes even our good friends into our competitors, our enemies, at least in our own minds. If I didn't have a neighbor, someone whom I can observe in proximity and lay alongside my life, I would have no object of Envy. It is not only the dumb barnyard chickens that have pecking orders. To be human is to be in community, and to be in community is to be in hierarchy, a pecking order in which one constantly positions and repositions oneself in relationship to others. One puts on robes, wears a miter, a cope, and carries a crook and says that one does this for purposes of "servant leadership." Well, you get the point.

Perhaps humanity could have gotten by without Envy, but when Eve "bore a second son" and there were two of us in the world, we were bound to be joined by Envy. As Cain found out with Abel, it is very difficult to urge people to be social and fraternal, without also urging them to measure themselves, to define their self-worth on the basis of others. We did not need the post-Freudians to tell us that birth order is a major factor in the tension among siblings: the Bible managed to show the ravages that Envy works in families with Cain and Abel, Joseph and his brothers, Jacob and Esau, and others. Though I don't believe those who say that the Arab terrorists are against us because they "envy our freedom," I do believe that Envy of something has everything to do with their hatred. Envy between nations is a cause of many wars.

With all the high-sounding, *au courant* appeals to nurture "community" among us distinctly individualistic Americans, I expect a concomitant outbreak of Envy. The truly self-sufficient individualist, if there is such a human animal, ought to be immune from Envy; the truly gregarious communitarian, never.

We need not be surprised that the Seven Deadly Sins were noted, defined, and reiterated among those who knew the peculiar demands of the monastic life. It would take a person closely confined with others in a convent or monastery to know the ravages of Envy. When you lived with everyone in identical uniforms, you all ate exactly the same food, and you all slept on the same beds, all equal before God, Envy was inevitable as a means of groping for some individual distinction—noting a particularly prideful demeanor, a certain haughty tone of voice, that indicated someone's incipient Pride, and therefore made someone a source of Envy. Perhaps this is why Envy is found so often on college faculties where professors, living in such limited and confined space, and there being little economic rewards to fight over, must fight over something. So they fight over tenure or parking or titles, anything to suggest that one person is better than another.

Envy works best at close range. Hume noted that rarely do we envy those who are much, much greater than ourselves. Envy breeds on "proximity."[2] Kierkegaard, who wrote about as much on the subject of Envy as any theologian, wrote in *The Sickness Unto Death* that Envy is a small-town sin, a by-product of living so close to a set of other people that one is constantly tempted to make leveling comparisons. Those who are too far above you are so far above you that you cannot imagine yourself in their position. Why should I envy the achievements and acquisitions of Bill Gates? His world is so far beyond my reach as to be irrelevant. But the pastor down the street at St. Luke's at the Country Club Church—that's a horse of a different color, closer to my color, fit subject for comparison. Though the poet Auden advised (in his poem "Many Happy Returns") to "love without desiring all that you are not," a romp through Auden's letters shows that he really had it in for some of his fellow poets.

In his *Summa*, Aquinas notes that "Envy is an offspring of

vainglory." Aristotle states that "those who love honor and glory tend more to Envy." This suggests that Envy thrives among those who are ambitious. Those who set high sights for themselves invariably have others in their sights, somebody at the top whom they would like to supplant. Yet, as we said, Envy is perhaps more the small-town, petty sin, the sin of small people, people who seem small precisely because of their Envy.

I don't know if this is any comfort or not, but in my experience, contrary to popular prejudice, Envy is an equal-opportunity employer: men and women are equally envious. I've never met a woman yet who envies what Freud accused her of envying. Envy seems most often to be a same-sex sin. Men tend to Envy what men have or are, and women appear to do much the same regarding other women. It all begins in the showers after the junior high basketball game.

But enough of that. Sir Philip Sidney, in *Arcadia*, claims, "Those who have true worth in themselves, can never Envy it in another."[3] But how could there be someone who has "true worth in themselves"? How would you know "true worth" when you got it if you had not measured your worth by some external means? Besides, is there any great quality that we can have solely on our own, by ourselves? It seems ridiculous for the solitary individual simply to announce that he has "true worth" regardless of what anyone else thinks. Our "true worth" is a social construction. Envy is a fruit of our social life.

As Duke University entered into the NCAA Basketball Tournament a few years ago, I was struck, when people were interviewed on television, by how deeply they hoped that Duke, the favorite, would not win the championship. As someone said, "Everybody loves an underdog." Why? Is it because we all know ourselves to be underdogs, inferior when measured against someone else, and we long to see the underdog win, hoping that we ourselves might eventually win?

Duke did not win the championship that year, for what it was worth. I can tell you, in regard to the team that beat us, that any Envy we might have felt at their victory was almost instantaneously transformed into contempt for their inferiority and their undeserved and inexplicable luck at beating a clearly superior team like us!

When I told our former athletic director at Duke that, in my travels about the country, I heard many compliments for our "clean athletic program," he surprised me by saying, "Don't tell me that! Now people will really be out to get us!"

When my neighbor bought a Lexus, for at least a year he made sure to arrive home each evening under the cover of darkness and took care always to park in his garage lest he provoke my Lexus Envy. He did not succeed.

The saints have unanimously told us to shun competitive posturing, to relate ourselves only to God, as a remedy against Envy. The Pharisee was talking only to God when he prayed, in Luke 17, "God, I thank thee that I am not like other men, adulterers, thieves, etc., such as that tax collector over there...." The Pharisee demonstrates how very difficult it is to say much to God without saying something about our relationship to others, and, as we have noted, our relationships with others have been characterized, since Adam and Eve's brood, by Envy. Jesus promises us that wherever two or three are gathered, he is there. And wherever two or three are gathered, it is hard to imagine there being an absence of a third by the name of Envy.

Somewhat shamelessly, I say to you that I cannot think of a time that I have succumbed to the sin of Envy. Rather than see others as rivals, challengers to my self-respect, I generally am pleased to tend to my own garden because, in comparison to their garden, mine looks fairly good. Now, I would like to tell you that my lack of Envy is due in some large measure to my virtue. Unfortunately, my disinclination toward Envy most probably stems from a surfeit of Pride. I do not see those as rivals whom I regard as my inferiors. Then again, perhaps my sense of superiority is some sort of compensation for my secret Envy of them? It is hard to say for sure because, in my experience, Envy is the most secretive of the Seven and the one sin we are most likely not to admit. Joseph Epstein says that envious people tend to go in for irony (I love to use irony in sermons) and scorn (I'm guilty, on occasion) as a cover for their Envy. Epstein quotes Leslie Farber, who says, "Envy has a talent for disguise" (p. 11).

Jesus told a parable about some workers who showed up early in the day to labor in the vineyard, while others showed up later in the morning, at midday, even one hour before quitting time (Matthew 20). At the end of the day, the quixotic landlord paid everyone the same wage. There was grumbling from those who had sweated in the fields all day, yet who received the same wage as those who had only been there for an hour. The landowner feigned surprise. "Why are you envious because of my generosity?" he asked. Or, closer to the Greek, "Why is your eye evil (*opthalmos poneros*), because I am good?" Why begrudge the master's generosity?

I'll tell you why. Those of us who have been lifelong Christians, attempting to follow Jesus from our youth, bored to tears for decades in Sunday school and long sermons, why should we not be envious when some little wayward lamb staggers back to the sheepfold, or some once Prodigal Son turns back toward home? Our God is gracious, forgiving, abounding in mercy. Grace, mercy, and forgiveness, when they are offered to you, can be just as envied by me, even more envied, than cars, money, and power. Grace, when it is so freely offered to any and all comers, without regard to my merit, especially when offered to latecomers, seems somehow less gracious than when it is reserved for me.

The first murder, a fratricide, that trouble between Cain and Abel, was due to Envy at the gracious love of God showered on a brother. Some animosity among religious people could be chalked up to the childish "my God is better than yours" attitude, but I wonder if some of that enmity is due to the "your god seems oddly more beneficent than mine" attitude. I expect that the blessings of God have led to more head bashing than any other source of Envy. Why God blessed the heathen Arabs with all that oil, I will never know.

I doubt you will be surprised when I say that, for me as an aging male, I would rather be lusted after than envied. I would rather be too fat than to be too envied for my thinness. To be the object of another's Envy is a most unenviable position to be in. The person who comes into a great inheritance will likely receive that inheritance with a large measure of embarrassment and attempt

to keep it secret. It's not due to modesty. This person knows well
the ravages of the Envy of others. Wilde's Lord Illingworth noted,
"A title is really rather a nuisance in these democratic days. As
George Harford I had everything I wanted. Now I have merely
everything that other people want" (Oscar Wilde, *A Woman of
No Importance*, 1893). As Nietzsche once noted (in *All Too
Human*), we owe many of our best friends to the fact that we have
given them, in our lives, so little to Envy. Australians sometimes
pride themselves on their alleged national effort to rein in the sin
of Pride by exercising what they call "the tall poppy syndrome"—
a person who sticks out too far from the herd will be eagerly put
down by the rest. Sounds like a recipe for mediocrity.

Our expression "green with Envy" denotes that historically
Envy has been personified as a sickly person. There are some sins
that make others ill. Envy debilitates its host. Indeed, of all the
sins, Envy seems to be its own punishment. In envying another,
my self is diminished, continually diminished every time I make
the invidious comparison. Thus Ovid (in *Metamorphoses*, Book
2) depicts Envy as wasting away at a cave, cankerous and sick. In
Shakespeare's *Merchant of Venice* (Act 3, Scene 2) Portia speaks
of "green-eyed jealousy." I am just sick that I envy my neighbor's
Lexus. I am loath to admit to myself or to my neighbor that my
neighbor is greater than I.

Aquinas's depiction of Envy as a mode of sadness is revealing.
I can imagine someone enjoying Gluttony, at least until the
morning after, and Lust surely carries with it its momentary pleasure. But Envy? It is hard to imagine someone relishing Envy or
receiving much pleasure from it. Surely we instinctively know

that to envy others, to feel ourselves diminished by their achievements, is a way of constantly reminding ourselves that we really are lesser mortals than they.

Some would attempt to rehabilitate Envy into an engine for achievement. I know a woman, an African American, who served as a domestic servant in a rich woman's house. Her experience of that woman's fine things made her desire fine things as well. She left domestic work and founded a janitorial service company. When asked, "How have you achieved so much?" she replied, "I wanted what rich people had so bad that I went out and got some of it for myself."

But I have rarely observed the positive effects of Envy. Envy seems to debilitate rather than energize. Envy is rarely a positive motivation because it usually ascribes someone else's accomplishments to fickle fortune or to their schmoozing up to others in order to get rewards, rarely to the other person's innate abilities or hard-won achievements. Rather than say, "I'll get busy and I'll show you," too often Envy is content with merely saying, "You are certainly not as great as other people think you are. I could do as well as you, if I wanted, but I wouldn't lower myself to be like you."

A professor I know, when hearing of a colleague being given a prestigious history award, said, "I could sell as many books as he, if I didn't have such high standards for my scholarship." I recall another academic who, upon learning of the recipients of the Nobel Prize for Chemistry, commented, "Sweden is a pitifully small country."

Not long ago, when visiting a nearby campus, I met with the

acting dean of the faculty. I asked him, "How have you enjoyed being a dean?" He replied only, "Why can't people just be happy with what they've got?"

After more than twenty years of undergraduate and seminary teaching, I would say that our greatest challenge, as faculty, is not Envy of those who win Nobel Prizes (again, Envy needs realistic competitors to despise). The greatest discipline needed by faculty is to resist Envy of the young. When your life is gradually winding down, their lives are gearing up. Students are young, well-futured; faculty are old, on our way out. After my experience of being an old person amid young people, I predict that in our culture you will hear more and more about friction between the generations. We Envy their future; they resent our past. They think we're gobbling up their social security; we suspect they will stash us away at Shady Acres Rest Home once they get the chance.

In his *Rhetoric*, I was surprised to hear Aristotle speak of emulation as a good sort of Envy, Envy that folds into admiration and gives birth to imitation of the virtues that we Envy (oops, I mean "admire") in another. Far be it from me to go against Aristotle, but that seems to put too positive a spin on a sad, sick sin. To feel Envy at the achievements of others, even their moral achievements, is, in the words of the *Oxford English Dictionary's* definition of *envy*, to be gripped with "the feeling of mortification and ill will" in thinking of another person's life when compared with your own.

That curious emotion *Schadenfreude*—perverse delight in the failures and misfortunes of others—is a sibling of Envy. That sin that prohibits us from rejoicing at the achievements of others prods us to rejoice at their failures. Whereas most of our Envy leads us to ask, "Why not me?" *Schadenfreude* occurs on those occasions when we say to ourselves, "Thank God it's him and not me!" The great Schopenhauer explained it thus: "Because they feel unhappy, men cannot bear the sight of someone they think is happy."[4] The most often cited word on *Schadenfreude* is La Rochefoucauld: "In the misfortune of our best friends, we always find something that is not displeasing to us." *Schadenfreude* has got to be Envy's nastiest side.

We were all just a bit too gleeful in the demise of Martha Stewart, a fabulously rich woman who kept her house better than we kept ours. To have this uppity woman slide into the hands of the district attorney, this was wonderful, *Schadenfreude* at its most delicious. Enjoy the feast, for someday we may wake up and realize that our righteous celebration in Martha's fall may reveal more of our moral weaknesses than hers, an eating away at our souls due to Envy.

In "Snow White" the evil queen asks, "Mirror, mirror, on the wall, who is the fairest of them all?" It is not enough for Envy merely to achieve a status of attractiveness; it wants to be the most attractive of all. This sort of comparison is bound to lead to lives of great disappointment. Envy sometimes sets unrealistic goals for itself and then pays in its eternal sense of frustration.

I would guess that at least eighty percent of our criticisms of others have their roots in Envy. The fox in Aesop's fable devalues the grapes in order to console himself for not being able to reach them. Those of us who are not particularly wealthy really need to believe that rich people are miserable. Sour grapes. The kid who does not do particularly well in school condemns those "nerds" who do. The moral failure really needs to believe that the saint is a self-righteous, Bible-beating prig.

"Envy" says Adam Smith, "is that passion which views with malignant dislike the superiority of those who are really entitled to all the superiority they possess."[5] Envy goes beyond the passivity of mere resentment at the achievements of others, or joy at their failures. Envy can also be an active conspirator in the downfall of others. Dr. Samuel Johnson felt that Envy was much worse than selfishness. The glee with which some people condemn the errors of others, a glee that is often far out of proportion to the magnitude of their own errors, as well as their subtle attempts to derail the good that others would do, stems from, according to Dr. Johnson, "The satisfaction of poisoning the banquet which they cannot taste, and blasting the harvest which they have no right to reap."[6]

Thus I came to understand what seemed to me the essentially irrational actions of a fellow faculty member in blocking, circumventing, and doing everything possible to derail a project of a fellow faculty member who would have undoubtedly contributed to the betterment of our school. If I cannot achieve this good, why should I help you achieve it? Envy that promotes a kind of ethical passivity is bad; active Envy is worse.

My wife does not need to think long and hard to figure out why I condemn Tom Cruise as a very bad actor. Freud knew all about this sort of thing. In fact, Freud made Envy the engine that drives the human machine. From the Oedipal little boy, envying Dad's relationship to Mom, to the (supposedly) self-hating woman envying the powerful male, Freud thought that Envy is at the heart of much of what we do. Name it, note it, and live with it rather than futilely try to get over it, advised the doctor of Vienna. Freud is probably the one most responsible for the modern tendency to regard Envy as a perfectly natural, utterly pervasive human tendency, not a sin. While Envy might be the most pervasive of the Seven (though I may not be guilty of Lust or Gluttony, I still don't like to see others eat or fornicate too well), I think it represents us at our most vile, not at our most "natural." Envy is serious.

Envy is also extremely difficult to tame. It is not good enough to urge someone never to measure oneself by others, to compete only with oneself. When there is no one to blame but yourself, you are in a very vulnerable position. When I am my own best friend, or my own most severe critic, why get out of bed in the morning? Nobody to talk to but me.

Is there any pleasure to be had in being the object of Envy? Envy by one's enemies is bitter. But there is this sort of sweetness in being envied by one's friends. When told that a fellow clergyman "despises you because you got that great pulpit," I was not overly saddened. When I looked at my new job, I saw great tasks and great risks, but this person saw it as incredible, undeserved, unadulterated good fortune. I thought more highly of my new job.

That said, you do well to be suspicious when I tell you that someone else feels animosity toward me out of Envy for my achievements. There are times when the sin of Pride, my Pride, trumps the possibility of someone else's Envy. There is something more than a tad delightful in thinking that someone, particularly someone whom I consider to be my inferior, lies awake at night just green with Envy of my life. Snobbery is a cousin of Envy.

Thus the sickness of Envy tends always to get worse, to develop complications, to beget a host of other even less attractive and perhaps more deadly sins. Aquinas, in article 4 of the *Summa*, notes that Pride is the father of vain ambition and that it gradually warps the soul toward Envy. "Gregory says that the capital sins are so closely connected that one comes from another. The first offshoot of pride is vainglory, and this, by eating away at the afflicted soul, soon begets Envy. When the mind craves the prestige of an empty name then it also repines for fear lest someone else should be accorded it." The deadliness of the Seven is often in their combined, cumulative effect upon the soul rather than in their individual badness.

In a televised, global world, poverty is especially degrading because the poor are constantly bombarded with images of those who are better off than themselves. There was a time when the common folk had no idea of how lavishly royalty lived. But I've been in the Queen's living room more times than I can count, thanks to TV. It really grates on me that this woman has what she has through absolutely no effort or virtue of her own.

Conservatives from de Tocqueville to Richard John Neuhaus have reassured us that most demands for justice and equality are usually nothing more than expressions of Envy. Nietzsche chalked up the French Revolution to nothing but envious class hatred. People on the left, so the argument goes, merely want to drag everybody down to their mediocre level. Most people I know on the left say that they want to raise up those who are worst off, not drag down those who are well off, but who knows? George Bernard Shaw put it acerbically: "Class hatred is not merely a matter of Envy on the part of the poor and contempt and dread on the part of the rich. Both rich and poor are really hateful in themselves. For my part I hate the poor and look forward eagerly to their extermination. I pity the rich a little, but am equally bent on their extermination."[7]

When it comes to who is the most envious in politics—the socialists with their attempts to level society or the capitalists with their systems of economic striving and reward—I think it's a draw. True, the Marxists murdered millions in their utopian desire to create the society in which all reasons for Envy would be eliminated. In my experience of Marxist societies, they did not overcome Envy but exacerbated it with their faceless, featureless bureaucracies. When everything is coercively leveled and all are legislated to be equal, then Envy really kicks in.

Also, by its nature, Envy is big on keeping score, assessing the relative worth of things, justice. In my experience, many of those on the left, including those on the left in the church, are big on "justice," which means that they tend to be even more concerned with "injustice." Envious people tend to be obsessed with justice. And even so noble a man of justice as Immanuel Kant worried, in *The Metaphysics of Morals*, about crusaders who, under the guise of concern for the good of others, are "intent on the destruction of the happiness of others." Yet great inequalities in wealth and material goods, as I noted earlier in my comparison of myself with Bill Gates, do not tend to excite us as much as relatively small inequalities—when my next-door neighbor gets a new car. So I don't believe that most of the socialists' love of social engineering is attributable to Envy.

On the other hand, the capitalists gave us advertising, which would be silent without cultivating the sin of Envy. When Adam Smith extolled the "invisible hand" of the Market, I think he was mostly talking about the engine of Envy, though he did not admit it. As Joseph Epstein puts it, "Under capitalism, man envies man; under socialism, vice versa."

In 1 Corinthians 13, Paul says that love, Christian love, does not envy. He wouldn't be preaching against Envy if it were not a problem in the church. Yet, in extolling the primacy of self-giving rather than self-seeking love, Paul points the way to a vision of a world in which Envy, the most natural thing in the world, is transformed, in which our selves are reformed by Christ's love for us. That new world is called the church, church as it is meant by God to be.

Aquinas refers love for neighbor to our love for God. He argues, in article 6 of the *Summa*, that "hatred of neighbor would then be referred to hatred of God." Why? Because our God is our neighbor's God too, our neighbor's Creator and Father; to hate our neighbor is to hate the God who gave us the neighbor. Although Aquinas doubts that Envy is the child of hate, by implication, to Envy our neighbor's goods is not only to despise ourselves but also to despise God. To regard our lives as diminished, in comparison with our neighbor's life, is to despise the God who gave us our lives as they are. It is to say that God made a mistake in making us as we are, in giving us the gifts that we have been given, and by implication, in making our neighbor and giving our neighbor the gifts that have been given.

While Aquinas finds it impossible to believe that we could envy God, "since we do not envy those who are at a maximum distance from us but those who are near, as Aristotle says," I expect that, even in our dealings with one so exalted as God, there is Envy. Why can't we have the power to run the world as it ought to be run? Why doesn't God move as quickly as we would move if we were God? More to the point of the Seven, why did God not use the good judgment to create us as gods unto ourselves rather than as the frail, finite creatures we are? Our Envy is evidence that we are not created as we wish we had been; therefore, by implication, our Envy is evidence of the creative mistakes of the Creator.

Seen in this light, Envy becomes more theologically interesting than at first it appeared to be.

Note: As I was finishing these thoughts on Envy, my wife called to tell me that an acquaintance of mine has just been given a prestigious, lucrative honor. Not that I have sought this honor for myself, but still, it is not beyond the realm of possibility that I might have received this particular honor, and the cash involved. Although I certainly, through my untiring and unselfish efforts, deserved this honor far more than he, I could never have lowered myself to his sycophantic, groveling, unctuous efforts whereby this honor came to him. The little brownnose.

The reader is hereby advised to disregard what I said earlier about my Envy immunity. The green-eyed monster has got me too.

CHAPTER FOUR

ANGER

A nger is a self-evident sin. Who wants to be the "angry young man" or the "angry radical feminist"? When there is an angry outburst, we say, "I lost it." In Anger we feel that we have lost something of our humanity. The mark of the well-developed, controlled, and refined human being is magnanimous moderation, not Anger. The temper tantrum is the mark of the spoiled brat. And who wants to be labeled as either spoiled or a brat?

And yet the Gospels say that, on Palm Sunday when Jesus marched in triumph into Jerusalem, the very first thing he did was to walk into church and, with whip in hand, violently drive the money changers from the Temple. Calling church officials a "gang of thieves," turning over the tables, scattering the coins, and screaming, "Zeal for my Father's house has consumed me." Not one of Jesus' best moments.

Or is it? Sorry, if all you know about Jesus was that he was nice to little children and considerate of lilies, the first act of this Holy Week drama is Jesus' Anger. The first thing he does is to clean up the church before he goes to die. Here is righteous indignation personified. Before Jesus is forgiving of us, Jesus is angry with us. He comes to church, takes whip in hand, and commands, "Get out of here!"

It is not only his Anger, but also the object of his Anger, that troubles me. Of course, I'm clergy, the professionally religious, just the sort of profession that Jesus appears to have despised. I note that this rare display of christological Anger is not vented at the politicians, the military-industrial establishment, Tyco executives, Michael Jackson—the folk who make me mad. He is angry with the folk in the Temple, God's people, the religious, us. How does it feel to meet God's wrath and judgment before meeting God's grace? Many biblical scholars believe that Jesus was crucified, in great part, because of this scene in the Temple. And I believe them. Anger is that emotion that, when engaged against us, makes us, well, *angry*.

Much of the bad that happens in the Bible occurs as a by-product of Anger. In resentful Anger, Cain killed Abel. The first time the Bible mentions rage, that fraternal rage leads to the first fratricide. In Anger, Jonah refused to obey God's call to go to Nineveh, and fled in the opposite direction to Tarshish. Jesus' first sermon, at his hometown synagogue in Nazareth, ended in Anger. They tried to kill him, so enraged were they by his words.

I once asked a police officer, "What causes you the most fear in your work as a policeman?" He said, "Anger is my greatest fear." He didn't fear burglaries, muggings, embezzlements. There, "nobody has anything against anybody." The bloodiest crimes are usually domestic—crimes of passion, as we put it. He said that when Anger is the cause of the crime, things get horribly, terribly bloody. He went on to say that, as a police officer, he also feared Anger in himself. "I have to keep saying to myself, and to the perpetrators whom I arrest, 'I'm just doing my job,' or 'This isn't personal.' The minute I get emotionally involved, the time when I think too much about the crime or the criminal, then I'm apt to get angry and then I am apt to do some very bad things myself."

So I don't have to make a great case, in my reflections with you upon Anger, to number Anger as one of the deadliest of the Seven Deadly Sins. You know that we are at our worst when we are most angry.

And yet, even moderate, balanced, and reasonable Plato had to admit that mere reason is inadequate motivation for human engagement for good. Reason helps us avoid doing wrong, but reason lacks the energy to motivate us to do good. Even Plato said that in order to know a subject, one must become "erotic" about it. Eros, desire, is not all bad. In order to know something at its deepest level, one must be able to fall in love with the subject. In dealing with an emotion like Anger, it's not good enough to say, "Don't be emotional." We are created by God to be passionate, caring, and feeling animals.

When asked, "What characteristic do you most want to see in seminarians?" the dean of our divinity school answered, "Passion."

I sat there thinking, "Passion? Aren't we clergy supposed to be against passion?"

No. There is no real engagement with a subject, no real growth and development, when all we bring to the table is apathetic detachment. Which brings us immediately to the paradoxical quality of Anger. Much of the greatest good worked in the world is through Anger. You can't say that about any of the other Seven.

As we consider Anger, let's admit that we tend to think of the Christian faith in a platonic fashion. Christianity sooths ruffled feathers. Christians are those who, from training over a lifetime, know how to sit quietly and listen.

I think of all those well-meaning parents who enter the church on Sunday, attempting to moderate their young children's voices with, "Shush! Now's the time for church voices! No loud talking. Church voices."

But the man who said, "Moderation in all things," was a pagan philosopher like Plato, not Jesus. Jesus wept for the fate of his beloved Jerusalem and justified his loud, angry, passionate voice in the Temple by appealing to God-given, unbridled zeal. On the cross he cried out in wild despair. If you read the Bible, listening in on the conversations between Israel and God, you will discover that conversations between this God and God's people quickly get overheated. As the Bible often says, our God "is a jealous God." This God is not a cool, dispassionate, and detached bureaucrat, just following the rules, treating everyone without regard or engagement. The God of Israel and the church is a passionate lover, a God who has staked a great deal upon us, who cares deeply about us, risks all for us, and demands the best of us. In short, just the sort of God who would get white-hot mad with us for making such a mess of things at God's Temple.

Not long ago, I participated in a scholarly conference on "prophetic ministry today." In lectures and discussions we explored the history of the prophets in eighth-century Israel, current issues in prophetic thought, biblical dimensions of prophecy, and so forth. During one of the last discussions, a young man rose, a student. He was shaking all over and shouting at the top of his voice into a startled hall of academics, "Do you people know what Israel is doing in the occupied territories? I've just gotten back from a month in Ramallah, and terrible, horrible things are happening there! I can't believe that you sit here and have these dumb discussions when something that bad is going on there...." On and on he went in his rant.

I thought that his rage was a rather remarkable moral achievement. This young man was a senior. He had been in academia for most of his life. Academia is that world where we teach students to step back, stay cool, keep emotions in check in order to use only reason, calm deliberation, and thoughtful moderation. I can't believe that, after being in college for four years, he was still able to get worked up over something.

A couple of years ago, at the end of one of our noon services during Holy Week, a faculty member at the divinity school, a visiting faculty member from another country, came up to me and, shaking all over, jaw set, lower lip trembling, said to me, "Are you completely unaware of what your country is doing? Invading other countries, killing civilians, destroying homes in Iraq while we sit here and prattle on about sentimental, spiritual trivialities!"

I reminded him that we were in church and that was not a proper tone of voice to use with clergy.

As a pastor, I have grieved over those people—usually women—who suffer some great injustice and who handle it by turning that pain inward upon themselves rather than toward its proper object, the perpetrator of the pain. There are those who think that Christians are not allowed to be angry. If you are Christian, you'll always be all smiles.

I'm thinking of the woman whose husband left her, without word of warning, after two years of marriage. She was terribly depressed. I asked her, as her pastor, "Are you angry that your husband has done this to you?"

"No," she replied, "not really angry, just hurt."

"Not angry?" I asked. "I think you've got a right to be angry with him. And maybe angry with God, also. After all, God told you to be faithful in your marriage vows and you were. But the other side of the bargain wasn't kept. I would think you would be angry!"

"No, just hurt," she said. I decided then and there that depression is often the result of Anger turned inward, Anger inappropriately expressed, Anger suppressed.

I told her to go home and read Psalm 137 at least once a day for a week, then come back and we would talk.

John Wesley was probably thinking of Psalm 137 when he commented that "there are some psalms that are unfit for Christian ears":

> Remember, O LORD, against the Edomites
>   the day of Jerusalem's fall,
> how they said, "Tear it down! Tear it down!
>   Down to its foundations!"
> O daughter Babylon, you devastator!
>   Happy shall they be who pay you back
>   what you have done to us!
> Happy shall they be who take your little ones
>   and dash them against the rock! (Psalm 137:7-9)

These are not nice sentiments. "Happy shall they be who take your little ones and dash them against the rock"? Such white-hot, vicious Anger, and in the Bible?

Before you judge harshly these ancient forebears in the faith, a couple of points to ponder: though I have never once had a desire to bash in the head of anyone's baby, I have never seen my little ones led to the gas chambers. The psalm does not say that the singer of the psalm is going to dash anyone against a rock. The psalm simply says that, if we had a just God who ran the world as God ought, then God ought to dash the evil, destructive Edomites' young against a rock. I believe that this is the psalm of those who are victims of unjust violence—the exiles who had seen their beloved city destroyed—not the song of those who go forth to do violence.

What does one do when one is the victim of injustice? One can contort the face and weep. And that is fine, as far as it goes. One can seethe in vindictive resentment, awaiting the day when one can work vengeance in some fashion. And then one can clench the fist and cry out to God for vindication.

This is the "Father, into thy hands I commend my spirit" that Jesus uttered from the cross. Most of the time, we think of these words of Jesus as resignation. But perhaps they were spoken in defiance, as Jesus' noble giving things over to his Father.

From Psalm 137 we obtain some insights for godly dealing with Anger: Anger is a natural, necessary response in the face of injustice. It is an acknowledgment that this is not the world as it is meant to be, not the world as God intended. The Anger should be expressed, preferably in church, in prayer, in conversation with God. We have a God who is good enough and great enough to receive our Anger, to take even the most raw human emotions and weave them into his purposes. Anger can be expressed, but ought not be acted upon without the greatest of care. "Vengeance is mine," says the Lord, not ours. Gross injustice, great Anger, ought to be given to God as our offering, our confession that we have come to a place in our lives where we are unable to fix that which afflicts us.

After two sexual assaults on our campus, the next evening hundreds of students streamed silently out on campus, in front of the chapel, and, at the signal, stood there and screamed. They had a "scream-in." Nobody proposed a plan of action, a program of campus betterment, a strategy. They just stood there and, in righteous rage and indignation, screamed. I thought it was appropriate. It not only made those who screamed feel better but also reminded us of the horrible injustice of the world in which we live, a world to which too many of us become settled and accustomed. Rather than urging them to "calm down," I should be praying, "Lord, give us more righteous indignation." I wish that they had been free to bring their Anger into the church rather than stand outside the church.

Martin Luther extolled righteous Anger as the engine that drove him on to some of his very best work. "I never work better than when I am inspired by anger; for when I am angry I can write, pray, and preach well, for then my whole temperature is quickened, my understanding sharpened, and all mundane vexations and temptations depart."[1]

I know what Luther is talking about. When I was unjustly attacked (in my opinion) by a right-wing religious hate group, a victim of their hateful e-mails and venom, I sat down and wrote one of the most unfair, direct, fierce, unkind articles I've ever published. I thought it also one of my best. Anger is a powerful human motivating force for good, says Jesus as he boots the clergy out of the Temple.

And yet... Anger, in our hands, righteous indignation practiced by us, is a dangerous thing. Martin Luther's obscene denunciations of the Jews were written under the influence of Anger. Anger tends to drive us, not in prophetic zeal to right what's wrong with us and the world, but rather even deeper into ourselves, in seething, simmering resentment. Part of its sin is isolation. We are right; the world is wrong. We are victims of injustice; the world is unjust. Luther defined sin as "the heart all curved in on itself." Anger is famous for beginning with focus upon another and ending all curved in upon itself. If there is one thing worse than Anger enacted, it is Anger nursed, turned inward, fed, and nurtured.

I once taught a student who had been abused by her ex-husband. I heard her story the first day of class when she told me that, due to her history of abuse, she had trouble with men as professors. Then the class heard about her victimization at every opportunity. Repeatedly we heard of her continuing resentment at what this man had done to her. Ten years ago! I had the unpleasant task of telling her that if she could not do something about that Anger, she would never be able to function in ministry. There was no way that she could help others, until she first helped herself. I told her, "I never met your ex-husband and still I hate him—for his continuing abuse of you through the devastating effects of your Anger."

Anger protects the status quo of the ego. Anger isolates us, keeps us from having to be affected by the world around us, from having to change. Perhaps that helps explain why there are some people who appear to cling to their Anger, lovingly to refurbish and nourish their Anger, realizing that if they ever loose their grip upon Anger (or dared to try to break free of Anger's grip on them) they would be forced to be different.

In basketball, one must quickly put aside one's Anger at lousy officiating in order to function well in the next play. The poor player is the one who gets worked up over bad officiating or an opposing player rather than improving his own play.

Anger can be the great excuser. When a Vancouver hockey player maimed and nearly paralyzed for life a fellow hockey player, he appeared before the public and said he was sorry "for what happened." Note that he did not say, "I am sorry for what I did." We don't actually do these things. They just "happen."

Anger gets the best of us. We just "lose it." We have greater sympathy for the perpetrator who says, with a shrug of the shoulders, "What I said, I said in Anger. Sorry." Anger has a way of excusing us from responsibility. Once one is in the grip of white-hot Anger, once our indignation, righteous or otherwise, is kindled, who would expect us to do better?

From what I have observed, most people would choose Anger over grief, grief seeming to them more debilitating, and Anger appearing to allow some control over one's destiny. However, any control that Anger appears to give us, any empowerment, is illusory. I am inclined to believe that the sin of Anger depends upon frequency and its duration. Prolonged attachment to Anger is the bad thing, not the momentary bad-tempered outburst. Anger is the master that keeps us out of the world of others by locking us within ourselves.

"Never go to bed mad. Stay up and fight," advises Phyllis Diller.[2]

Bitterness comes from Anger that is not dealt with, Anger suppressed. Anger at least shows a welling up of passions, rather than sloth, which may be as deadly. Yet we seem in so many ways to have lost our capacity for righteous outrage.

The first word of Homer's *Iliad* is *menin*, which means "rage." "Sing, O goddess, of the rage of Achilles, son of Peleus." Rage gets things going. The *Iliad* is the bloody account of the results of rage enacted. For the early Greeks like Homer, Anger is a chief impulse of action, the source of great, heroic deeds, and a major reason for great tragedy. The Homeric hero walks a path between reserved cowardice and blind fury.

Plato said that our souls are like a charioteer who strives to control two horses, each pulling in a different direction. One horse is reason, the other is emotion. For Plato, the good soul learns to hold the reins in such a way that one horse (reason, of course) is dominant. The wise person learns to keep passion— emotions like Anger, rage, or desire—in check by the moderation of reason. Again we note that the one who said "moderation in all things" was not Jesus. Anger is that paradoxical sin which can be the engine that drives us on to do our best, or it can be that which incapacitates us and leads us to do our worst.

Perhaps all sins, or at least many of the Seven, are paradoxical. On the one hand, Anger can be righteous indignation at injustice; on the other hand, Anger can be that blind rage in which we see nothing but ourselves, and our diminished sense of self, reacting with murderous rage. Anger is surely one of the most self-delusional and destructive, usually self-destructive and potentially violent, of the Seven Sins. Therefore we ought to be careful, very careful, in ascribing any positive significance to Anger. We must be cautious in urging anybody to "let it all out."

Maybe that's why Scripture tells us, " 'Vengeance is mine,' says the Lord, 'I will repay.' " Vengeance, one of the most popular motivations for indignation, righteous or otherwise, is not a gift that God gives to us. Vengeance, the ultimate, final righting of what's wrong with the world, is God's business, not ours. Because our Anger can be so self-deceptive and delusional, so very dangerous to ourselves and to others, the church has called Anger a sin, and a deadly one at that. We are to guard against it, fight it with all our might, repress it, and stuff it in because, not being as wise or as loving as God, we are not to be trusted in our Anger.

This insight was given me by a woman I met in Belfast, Northern Ireland, a hard-working, devout Christian who does much good among the poor of that troubled city. I knew only that she was a widow and that she had recently remarried. When, in the course of our conversation, I asked her when her husband died, she replied, "He was murdered ten years ago."

"Murdered?"

"Right. I kissed him on the cheek as he left the house for work one morning, with our wee daughter at my knees. As he got into his car in front of our house a car pulled up, two men emerged, and one shot him five times in the face. The other shot at me, trying to kill me, but my daughter and I jumped back in the house and the bullets only shattered the door. Then they sped off. Paramilitaries, they were, IRA. My husband was a superintendent of a local jail and he was considered a fair target."

"That's just horrible," I said.

"It was horrible. They shot him up so bad, we were not able to let his dear mother see him before burial," she said.

"How on earth were you able to go on?" I asked her in amazement.

"Well, that very moment, as I stood there over his horribly bloody body, I started saying the Lord's Prayer. I got as far as 'Forgive us our sins, as we forgive the sins of others…' And I said at that point, 'Lord, you have forgiven so many of my sins, so I guess you expect me to forgive others of their sins. I will try to do that, but you'll have to help me every day not to be destroyed by anger. Every day.' And the Lord gave me that wonderful gift. I was able to forgive. I let God be angry with them, or punish them, or forgive them, or whatever the Lord chose to do with them. I chose to forgive. The gunmen killed one of the most wonderful men in the world, and none of them was ever convicted of the crime; but my anger was no match for God! God wouldn't let the anger of it all kill me!"

Because God in Christ gets angry with us and the world, we don't have to. We can go on, delivered of the horribly dangerous, terribly self-destructive sin of Anger.

So finally, once again in our exploration of the Seven, in talking about the sin of Anger we are not talking about us. We are talking about God-in-the-flesh Jesus. When Christians get together to pray, to talk, and to reflect, we tend not to talk about what we ought to do about ourselves and the world; we talk about what God is doing about us. Every time we look at the cross of Christ, it is not only a mirror of us at our worst, our angry, murderous worst; the cross is also a window whereby we are able to peer into the deepest mystery at the heart of God. When God had a grand opportunity to strike out decisively in justified vengeance against us, God majestically forgave us. The cross is God's great rebuke of us, that moment when God held up before us a mirror that reveals who we really are. And the cross is also when we got to see who God really is. God cares enough about us to get angry enough with us, and our sin, to forgive us.

On Golgotha God is judging us. God is smoking us out of our safe sanctuaries of communal and personal self-delusion. With whip in hand, God holds a harsh mirror of utter truth before us.

God is revealing our true selves in the mirror of the cross. Here, O church, is you at your very best. Look at yourselves.

He said, "Come to me."

And we with one voice cried, "Crucify him!"

But he refused to let our sin have the last word. To our "Crucify him!" he responded with, "Father forgive...."

Before Holy Week is done, there will be time for suffering with us and suffering for us, forgiveness of us and prayer for us, but along with this there is, as he drives us out of the Temple, Jesus' Anger against us so that he might be decisively for us.

CHAPTER FIVE

SLOTH

Sloth is a special case among the Seven Deadly Sins. Surely Sloth is one sin of which we pragmatic, hard-working, high-achieving, Mother-I'd-rather-do-it-myself Americans are not guilty. We are a purposeful, driven nation that resonated to Ben Franklin and his *Poor Richard's Almanac*: "Early to bed, early to rise" and all of that. (On the other hand, the phenomenal growth of state-sponsored gambling suggests that there are many of us who expect to be given a life for nothing, betting on luck, rather than hard work, to get what we want.) Once again we are faced with the challenge of naming something as a sin rather than a merely psychological disposition. If we think about Sloth, which is probably less thought about than any other of the Seven, it is not considered by us as a sin against God. Sloth is an offense against time, a sin against our potentiality, a sin against ourselves, a failure to get out there and grab what we deserve—in other words, our failure to become gods unto ourselves.

Acedia appears to be, among the Seven, a lightweight, even trivial.[1] Dozing off in the middle of the sermon, lying too long in the bath, is such behavior worthy of moral condemnation or even theological consideration? Perhaps I am being overly sensitive. Pastors have often been accused of Sloth, professors too. I recall asking an archaic Anglican clergyman what he thought to be the essential quality for a competent pastor and he said, "The grace to do nothing." True, the overachieving, relentlessly scheduled, busy pastor is probably not the sort of personality best suited for the reflective and prayerful aspects of the ordained ministry. Still, I wondered if the Anglican's parishioners extolled his inactivity as a virtue. As I recall, this particular clergyman's only real enthusiasm was for the collection and cataloging of butterflies.

Apathy could be a virtue. Voltaire commented that most of humanity's tragedies were the result of our inability to stay in our own room. Name me one war that has been fought by apathetic, slothful individuals. It's the overachieving, purpose-driven types who cause all of the problems. Back in the troubled 1960s, the comedian Pat Paulsen (who ran a bogus campaign for president), in a mock speech on TV, called for "a great, national groundswell of apathy" that would allow this nation to fall softly backwards into "peace, prosperity, and goodwill." Paulsen came to the crescendo of his speech but dribbled off into mumbling, "I don't really care whether any of you do this or not."[2]

One man asks another, "Don't you think that voter apathy is a real problem in this country?"

The other replies, "I don't know and I don't care."

Technology, like television, may aid and abet a slothful spirit, producing a nation of couch potatoes. We would rather watch athletic events than participate in them. We become the obese, too-much-time-on-our-hands victims of "labor-saving devices." But is this serious Sloth, and is Sloth serious?

Sloth as sin, Sloth seen as some sort of outrage against the goodness of God, is the peculiar contribution of the desert Fathers. In Scripture, it's the activist sins of commission, rather than the lazy sins of omission, that seem to be most troubling to God. Jesus had little to say in condemnation of folk who were slack in their religious commitments. It was the hard-working, eager-beaver, purpose-driven believers, the actively righteous who suffered his harshest rebukes.

I would expect Sloth would be thought a sin particularly by those committed monastic souls who left everything, turned their backs upon all the glittering images of this world, and ran away to God in the dusty desert. For those who were consumed with desire to have constant intercourse with God, what could be a greater betrayal of that desire than falling asleep at prayer?

Sloth—real, serious *acedia*—is the "noonday demon" described first by the Egyptian monks in the desert in the fourth century, occurring at that time of day when the hot sun is high and one cannot even see one's shadow. At such a time, one's existence is apt to seem insubstantial and inconsequential. These monks had seen firsthand the mighty Roman Empire decay to dust. So much for all of Rome's classical wisdom, architecture, and power. What good does it do us? Now these desert dwellers were on a venture to become citizens of a more enduring city, not like the decadent, imperial "Eternal City" made by human striving but an eternal *polis* built by God, using them as its building blocks. Prayer, fasting, study of the Scriptures would be the way toward this new empire of God that would conquer the world's decadent efforts at eternity. But now, in the searing heat of noon, eyes glazed over from too much scripture, stomachs growled, the city streets of Rome seemed more appealing, and the adventure of God seemed less adventuresome.

Any biblical justification for Sloth as a sin is in the backward glance, back from the rigors of living the Christian life to the scant attention to slothful disposition in the Bible. The only book of the Bible to do justice to that sense of ennui that is Sloth is the mournful Book of Ecclesiastes. "All is vanity. What do people gain from all the toil at which they toil under the sun? A generation goes, and a generation comes..." (Ecclesiastes 1:2-4). Go write your books, build your cities, perform even the best of good works and what does it get you? Dust, decay, and striving after the wind. One has to admire the compilers of scripture for the courage to stick a book like Ecclesiastes in the canon, a wonderfully sad and scornful minority report lodged against upbeat spiritualities of every stripe. Apathy is found here and just about nowhere else. That it is found here in Ecclesiastes is rather amazing. Even to admit to the presence of the apathetic disposition among the faithful is a rather threatening admission.

The monks took their main midday meal at three o'clock in the afternoon. At noon, the monk sitting in his cell began to get hungry. He got distracted from his prayers. His mind wandered, led astray by the noonday demon. In that wandering, surely he wondered, "What is the use of this holy effort anyway?"

There are those who think that tornadoes destroying towns, the suffering of little children, the wars in the world, and college religion courses taught by atheist professors are the chief threats to faith. I would nominate the less spectacular gradual attrition and erosion. The morning after a midnight visionary encounter with God is the great spiritual challenge. Among my parishioners, it is one thing to have a dramatic, life-changing conversion experience. It is quite another thing to keep it going over the long haul. Sloth eats away at the soul, extinguishes faithful fire, and thus takes its toll, wearing down the soul by slow degrees.

Sometimes Envy can be a prelude to Sloth, for the Seven tend to be interconnected. Aquinas, recalling the words of Cassian, says that Sloth arises "from the fact that we groan about not having spiritual fruit and we think that other, distant monasteries are better off than ours."[3] When I, as a beginner at the game of tennis, went to see Billy Jean King play an exhibition match, I quit tennis. Why humiliate yourself with failure to reach a goal that someone else so wonderfully masters?

In my pastoral experience, what people sometimes call doubt is more often, more properly called Sloth. Faith requires active response, engagement with God, a willingness to be formed and transformed by God's work in us. The Reformers were concerned not to make "faith" into a new form of "works righteousness," in which we attempt to save ourselves by ourselves. But today I wonder if the greater spiritual danger is that gradual dissipation of faith that comes from a simple unwillingness to take the trouble to believe.

Dante wisely places Sloth in the middle of his Purgatory, halfway up the mountain, or halfway down, depending on how you read it. It is in the middle of the day, the middle of life, that dangerous middle point when we have been on our way, and are halfway there, but not nearly there yet, sometime between noon and three, the same hours that Jesus hung on the cross, the same time of the afternoon when middle-aged King David awoke from his nap and spied the lovely Bathsheba at bath, that Sloth gets to us (2 Samuel 11–12). Sloth is that sin that is midway between all the things that drag us down in human life and all our attempts to pull ourselves out, that demon that jumps us at noon.

Aquinas links apathy with sorrow and with torpor:

> Damascene teaches that spiritual apathy *is a kind of oppressive sorrow* that so depresses a man that he wants to do nothing. Thus things that are acid are also cold. Spiritual apathy implies then a certain weariness about work. We know this from a gloss on the words of the psalm and *finding all food repugnant*, as well as from what others say, namely, that it is a *torpor of mind that cannot face getting down to work.*[4]

The only scriptural justification that can be mustered in behalf of making Sloth a sin comes from the Septuagint and Vulgate translations of the Bible, where the word *acedia* makes its sole appearance. In the apocryphal *Ecclesiasticus* (*Sirach*) 6:25, the faithful are advised to pursue holy wisdom by giving "your shoulder to the yoke and do not be restive in her reins (*et ne acedieris vinculis ejus*)." The failure to put one's shoulder to the task, that restiveness within the yoke of Christ, this is Sloth.

The desert Father John Cassian, writing about 420, eloquently describes the vice of spiritual apathy:

> Our sixth battle is with what the Greeks call *acedia* which we might name tedium or anxiety of heart. It is related to sadness, and is especially troublesome to hermits, a dangerous and frequent enemy to desert dwellers. It disturbs the monk especially at noon, like a fever recurring at regular intervals, bringing its burning heats in waves. Some of the ancients say it is the noonday devil of the ninetieth psalm.
> When it seizes some wretched mind, it begets a horror of his place, disgust with his cell and with the brethren. Every task to be performed seems to make him listless and inert. He cannot stay in his cell; it will not permit him to perform his duty of reading. He groans that he has made no progress after such a long time here. He complains and sighs: 'There is no spiritual fruit here, connected with this community; the whole spiritual quest has been in vain. To stay in this place is useless.' He is one who could govern others and be useful to a great number of people. Yet here he is edifying no one, nor profiting anyone by his teaching and doctrine. He cries up distant monasteries and those which are a long way off, and describes such places as more profitable and better suited for salvation; and besides this he paints the life there with the brethren as sweet and full of spiritual good. On the other hand, he says that everything about him is crude, and not only is there nothing edifying about his present brethren, but even necessary food is obtained with great trouble. Finally he imagines things will never go right while he remains there; unless he leaves his hermitage and gets away quickly, he will certainly die. Then the fifth and sixth hour brings such physical fatigue and hunger that he seems to himself worn out, wearied as by a long journey or some heavy work, or as if he has been fasting two or three days. Then he looks anxiously around, sighing that no brother ever visits him; he goes in and out of his hermitage, frequently looking up at the sun, as if it were too slow in setting. So a kind of

unreasonable confusion of mind like some soul-darkness takes hold of him, making him idle and useless for every spiritual work. He imagines there is no cure for so terrible an attack in anything except a visit to some of the brethren, or in the solace of slumber. Then the disease suggests he should show courteous and loving friendship to the others, pay visits to the sick, either near or far. He talks too about some dutiful and religious task; he should inquire about his relatives; he really ought to go see them more often; it would be a genuine work of piety to visit some religious woman who is devoted to God's service, yet deprived of all support from her family. It really would be a fine thing to get what she needs and does not get from her relatives. In fact, he really should piously devote his time to such affairs rather than wasting away uselessly here.

So the wretched soul, harassed by such contrivances of the enemy is disturbed until, simply worn out by the strong battering ram of his spirit of *acedia*, he sinks to rest, or, driven out of his confinement, gets in the habit of looking for consolation in these attacks in a visit to another brother, only to be later even more weakened by the remedy itself . . . who has become a deserter of warfare, involves himself in worldly business, and thus proves himself displeasing to Christ.[5]

I am very much attracted to the Fathers' notion of apathy as "a kind of sadness." Somewhere between white-hot, indignant anger and dramatic, tragic despair lies the sadness of *acedia*. On a modern university campus, with young adults so well funded, so well futured, so bright and full of potential, at any given moment, by my unscientific estimate, fully a third of them are depressed. More than a century after Cassian, Gregory the Great combined "sadness" (*tristitia*) and spiritual apathy (*acedia*) in his discussion of this sin. Sadness can be a good thing, a sense that life is not what it ought to be, a potential motivation to betterment, or it can be bad as an invitation to the downward slide toward complete despair.

Spiritual apathy's opposite is joy, particularly the joy that one has in the adventure of knowing and loving God. Apathy is despondency about God or, more precisely, a failure actively to believe that God is good and that God's goodness is for us. Apathy for the Fathers is not simply depression. It is that sad sin that leads us, when confronted by the gracious, open hand of God, to turn away. In Luke's story of Jesus and the Rich Ruler (Luke 18:18-25), when Jesus called the man (18:22) to be a disciple (and told him the requirements for discipleship), Luke says that "he became sad" (18:23), got depressed, and "turned away sorrowful." Or, as the old Authorized Version put it more vividly, "his countenance fell." He did not so much walk away from Jesus; rather he sorrowed that he did not have what it took to move toward Jesus. He could not bring himself to step toward the God who had moved toward him. This is closer to what the Fathers meant by *acedia* than mere languor or laziness.

Aquinas noted that behind the rather gray face of apathy lay a spiritual monster: despair. The great goal of life—communion with God—is forsaken by diving into a sea of triviality. The end of life is forfeited, and the means toward the end seem unrealistic and pointless. Failing to avail oneself of God's appointed modes of gracious ascent, we fall victim to malice and spite toward spiritual things, ridiculing the ways of the Spirit as we sink back into the ways of the flesh. "Wandering after illicit things" consumes our lives, resulting in a constant flux of mind in which we fail to alight anywhere. Idle curiosity, prattling, general restlessness, and instability fill our days.[6]

I have never completely recovered from a high school reading of Sylvia Plath's *The Bell Jar*. Her eloquent, utterly unflinching portrayal of depression and its effects is a rebuke to anyone's attempt to downplay apathy as a not-so-serious sin. Seriously to encounter someone in the grip of apathy at its worst is chilling. You would expect me to recall a scene that Plath describes when, while in college, a young man disrobed before her, seeking to entice her into an erotic encounter. Plath says that she blankly stared at him as he revealed his nakedness to her, and when he asked, "Well, what do you think?" all she could think of was "chicken necks." Eventually, after writing this book, she stuck her head in an oven, turned on the gas, and the world lost a great poet.

The opposite of Sloth is joy. Joy, real non-chemically and non–entertainment-induced joy, seems a rarity in our time. We are more into depression. Sloth is that couch-potato dullness where the eyes glaze over and the heartbeat slows to a thud, and the creative human made in the image of God becomes indistinguishable from the slug. Chrysostom could even say, "It is not so much sin but despair that casts us into hell."[7] You can see that sort of despair by looking in the eyes, as I did recently, of a group of inner-city high school students. Having had the door slammed in their faces so many times, they had developed the means not even to desire for the door to be opened.

Thomas notes that joy and zeal seem to arise from a confrontation with the beauty of things. Therefore beauty may be a kind of antidote to despair. The sheer ugliness of an inner-city school building is an invitation to despair. The French call apathy *ennui*, but I like the German *Weltsmerz*, literally pained by the world. For so many, it's the pain of the world that leads to Sloth as a defense against the world.

The frozen, zombielike stares among many Sunday congregations is a sort of evidence of despair. And also their roving eyes, their wandering minds. Distraction and restlessness of spirit are listed by the Fathers as aspects of apathy, failure to focus on what matters. We live in an age of a surfeit of distraction, of massive attention-deficit disorder. Failing to have our attention grabbed by anything of lasting value, our eyes, our minds wander, restlessly roving, failing to alight on anything worth having. And I'm no better than my congregation. My roving, wandering lack of attention to the Scriptures in my morning Bible study suggests the possibility, the frightening possibility, that when I cease to believe that the Bible speaks, and speaks to me, I cease to listen. Hildegard of Bingen speaks of sin itself as "drying up," a kind of desiccation of spirit.[8] This is what the Fathers meant when they said *apathy*.

In his painting *Sloth* in his *Seven Deadly Sins* in Museo del Prado, Madrid, Hieronymus Bosch (c. 1450–1516) depicts Sloth as a man sitting comfortably in a cushioned chair before a warm fire, his dog curled up at his feet, the very image of Dutch bourgeoisie contentment. A woman, seemingly a nun, holds out to him a rosary and a prayer book. But he contentedly sleeps. This is Sloth, refusing the God-given means to make our lives interesting.

Though they would not call it a "sin," Sloth is the favorite of those existentialist authors of the 1950s. They were the first to tell us that in a postindustrial, technological world, our defining emotion is despair, the inability to trust the future, the lack of faith in our ability to impact the present. Camus's *The Stranger* is a novel I have my freshmen read even today. It is the haunting account of a man, Mersault, who has withdrawn from the world, severed himself from life, unable to be touched by anyone and unable to be engaged by anything. "Mother died today, or was it yesterday?" is the novel's first line.

I have them read *The Stranger* because Sloth is the sin of today's college students, who not only fail to get the "big picture" after their studies in college, but also no longer even expect that there is a picture to be gotten from their studies. In general, Lust tends to be the sin of the young; despair is the sin of the aged, but not exclusively. I sit there, flailing away in a lecture, desperate to grab their attention, and they sit there, masters of the vacant state, eyes open, looking forward, living elsewhere, being nowhere. School is training in detachment, that ability to look upon all that the world has to offer—the history of ideas, the great achievements of Western Civilization, all the available options—and say, with a shrug of the shoulders, "I don't care."

Thus an identifying characteristic of today's college students is political apathy. Their failure to get involved in politics has something to do with their cynicism about our current crop of political leaders, but I think its basic cause is the students' loss of faith that anything they do, or anybody else can do, can make a difference. Cynicism—the world is rotten and I know it, so I'm checking out of the world as an active participant—is a close relative of apathy. And there is also, somewhat surprisingly, Pride.

I am too good, or too smart and perceptive, to get sucked into active engagement with life, unlike all those other suckers who are just setting themselves up for disappointment in the end. As the Fathers noted, all these sins are so closely connected.

When I was a student at Wofford College, so many years ago, they could kick you out not only for the usual sins, plagiarism, indiscretions with the opposite sex, habitual drunkenness, but also for what the administration called "failure to profit from a Wofford education." Even as a sophomore, I thought this an appropriate reason to kick somebody out of college. "Failure to profit" is a better reason for expulsion than drunkenness, which is stupidity, for which an undergraduate education ought to be a remedy. Failure to avail oneself of the means for an education, failure to live up to the sacrifices that have been made in one's behalf, failure to utilize the gifts that have been given, failure to trust in one's own abilities, such is the stuff of apathy.

Sloth is that sin that enables us to walk by the poor person with the outstretched hand, and no longer feel a twinge of conscience, no longer even see the empty hand reaching out to us in need, unable to consider the possibility that the man asking us for a handout is an invitation to get close to God. If asked, "What is your reason for walking past the one in need?" we reply, "No reason, really, just didn't see him, just can't bother."

Rather than call Sloth lazy, the Fathers defined it as excessive self-pity, a sad self-centeredness of the heart all curled up in itself, *Cor curvatus se*, which Luther said was the essence of all sin.

In Gethsemane (Luke 22:45), the disciples fell asleep while Jesus was in anguish. "Could you not watch with me one hour?" Jesus asks. Luke says that they fell asleep "because of grief," which has always struck me as the thinnest of excuses, one last attempt by Luke to make the disciples look better than they were. However, considering the Fathers' linkage of sorrow and Sloth, sadness and sleep, anguish and apathy, sleep is a believable apostolic response to the impending death of Jesus. In any number of parables, Jesus enjoins us to be awake, to be watchful. The Resurrection is the great awakening: "Awake, O sleeper and arise!" says Ephesians in what may be an early Christian baptismal hymn (Ephesians 5:14, paraphrased). Christians are those who, by the grace of God, awaken out of a slothful stupor and move toward the light. In Latin, *acedia* means sorrow, self-directed sorrow, feelings turned away from God and toward the self, that despair that comes from the sense that one is beyond God's help.

Sloth is therefore the sin of the somnambulant sinner who refuses to be forgiven, the arrogance of believing that one is without hope or help, the despair that there is no efficacy in the church's sacramental means of grace, the suspicion that when Jesus says, "Rise, your sins are forgiven," Jesus is lying.

Apathy is in part a feeling that God has not given us what we need to live this life well. In despairing over ourselves, we are ultimately despairing over God. It is one thing, says Aquinas, to be humble about your limitations, but it is sinful to be so humble about one's God-given gifts that one fails to use them. Says Thomas, "Humility is in that man who, knowing his own deficiencies, does not vaunt himself. But it is not humility, it is plain ingratitude, to condemn the gifts one has from God; and from such contempt spiritual apathy follows since we are sorrowful over things we think are bad and vile. We ought so to praise the blessings of others, as not to despise our own blessings provided by God. To do that would turn them into sorrows."[9]

In his account of his life, *The Education of Henry Adams*, Henry Adams describes the dissipation of religion from his cold, New England soul:

> Of all the conditions of his youth which afterwards puzzled the grown-up man, this disappearance of religion puzzled him most. The boy went to church twice every Sunday; he was taught to read his Bible, and he learned religious poetry by heart; he believed in a mild deism; he prayed, he went through all the forms; but neither to him nor to his brothers or sisters was religion real...they all threw it off at the first possible moment, and never afterwards entered a church. The religious instinct had vanished, and could not be revived.... The faculty of turning away one's eyes as one approaches a chasm is not unusual.[10]

That's the way the loss of faith was for proper Bostonian Brahmin Henry Adams. Faith ebbed away, without rage or passionate resistance, politely, slowly, but steadily until that day when faith was no more. One turns away the eyes from the emptiness within and the darkness without and just goes on. This is the failure of nerve that characterizes apathy's despair over God.

When asked about the demise of the modern novel, Flannery O'Connor replied,

> People without hope not only don't write novels, but what is more to the point, they don't read them. They don't take long looks at anything, because they lack the courage. The way to despair is to refuse to have any kind of experience, and the novel, of course, is a way to have experience.[11]

Modern people "don't take long looks at anything," says O'Connor, not necessarily because we are intellectually lazy, which we surely are, but because we "lack the courage." Darkness immobilizes, and it is possible, as a kind of defense, to move from feeling bad to refusing to feel at all.

I thought of O'Connor's judgment after finishing John Updike's *In the Beauty of the Lilies* (Knopf, 1996).[12] The novel is one of our most recent and eloquent literary depictions of apathy. *Lilies* chronicles the decline of an American family, beginning in a Presbyterian manse in Paterson, New Jersey, ending with a cult holocaust in Colorado reminiscent of the demise of the Branch Davidians in Waco.

Clarence Wilmot is a Princeton-educated preacher whose faith gradually ebbs away. When his scholarly Calvinism is spent, Wilmot is left with nothing with which to do business with the Almighty. Did Calvinism conceive a God so high, so lifted up and remote, that one day Calvin's heirs awoke to discover no one was there? More probably, the nineteenth-century Protestant liberal attempted to make moral and missionary activity substitute for mystery and revelation (much as many mainline Protestants now do), and he woke up one day with nothing but "God's inexorable recession."

It's all rather sad. But there's nothing to be done about it by Wilmot. Resignation is the only option. Perhaps that's why one form of Stoicism or another is the main competitor for the Christian faith in the modern, Western world, quiet, serene resignation, devoid of any passion or commitment. The Reverend Wilmot bows before the fact of God's demise. He doesn't protest or whine; he resigns himself to a silent, baffling universe that he no longer attempts to understand. Updike says, "In his present state he was a husk, depleted. . . ."

Wilmot is almost relieved after he at last admits that he no longer believes. "Oblivion became a singular comforter," says Updike. Now Wilmot, former pastor, former believer, former scholar, is at rest, secure in the knowledge of the "dismal hopelessness of human life." He dies quietly, slipping into the dark, "like an unmoored boat on an outgoing tide."

Why so peaceful, why at rest? There is a rest that comes from having gotten what our hearts desire. There is also rest that is given when desire dies. In other novels Updike's characters are passionate about nothing but sex, the major modern substitute for God, because they have lost desire for anything more interesting.

Evelyn Waugh called Sloth a primary late-modern sin.[13] A Christian theologian says of the sin of Sloth:

> The soul in this state [sloth] is beyond mere sadness and melancholy. It has removed itself from the rise and fall of feelings; the very root of its feelings in desire is dead. That is why, for the medieval moralist, sloth was...the most terrifying of sins. It is sin at its uttermost limit. To be a man is to desire. The good man desires God and other things in God. The sinful man desires things in the place of God, but he is still recognizably human, inasmuch as he has known desire. The slothful man, however, is a dead man, an arid waste . . . his desire itself has dried up.[14]

Sloth is thus a sort of slow, cowardly suicide.

The progeny of the Reverend Wilmot find some reason for living. A daughter loses herself in the materialistic excess and sexual fantasies of Hollywood. The son settles down into the comforts of a quiet, middle-class marriage. And the picture of our age grows more clear. Among us faith becomes, not faith in the God of Israel, but rather some vague, vapid, sentimental drivel about "the beauty of the lilies" out somewhere across the sea, remote from us, so remote a journey, and at such a cost, we dare not risk.

> I saw all the deeds that are done under the sun; and see, all is vanity and a chasing after wind.... I said to myself, "I have acquired great wisdom, surpassing all who were over Jerusalem before me; and my mind has had great experience of wisdom and knowledge." And I applied my mind to know wisdom and to know madness and folly. I perceived that this also is but a chasing after wind. (Ecclesiastes 1:14, 16-17)

Note that everything said here in Ecclesiastes is in monologue. There is no conversation with anyone outside the self. The self becomes exclusively self-constructed. "I said to myself . . ." No one is addressed outside the self. All is in vain. There is nothing but wind. Why bother?

The lives produced by contemporary Sloth may not be that interesting; certainly they are in no way heroic, as Updike's rather long novel shows. But at least they are at rest, at peace, having quit the battle, having retired to the tending of their own middle-class backyards, having nothing more to say to God, having no expectation of being addressed by anything or anyone outside themselves. In *The Road Less Traveled*, Scott Peck suggests that some people are judged to be "mentally ill" when in reality they are lazy, failing to move forward in life because they don't take the trouble. Mental health requires an active commitment to reality, says Peck.

Updike tells the saga of the Wilmots with such skill and charm that we are likely to sympathize with them, to sentimentalize their lapse into urbane disbelief, without recognizing their tragedy. But the novel is a tragedy of those who refuse to rage against the night. Disbelief ought to be made of sterner stuff.

A fellow pastor and I were discussing an outbreak of marital infidelities and sexual shenanigans among our parishioners. I lamented this rampant promiscuity among those who ought to know better. Yet he surprised me when he said, "For some of these folk, I'm almost glad to see them get passionate about something. My main job as a pastor is just to get them to care about something outside themselves." That remark certainly suggests that Sloth ought to be moved up the list of the Seven ahead even of Lust.

John Calvin said, "We are all made of mud, and this mud is not just on the hem of our gown, or on the sole of our boots, or in our shoes. We are full of it, we are nothing but mud and filth both inside and outside."[15]

As I said earlier—when you weren't paying attention and your mind was wandering and you had lost interest in my argument— the Book of Ecclesiastes says that of the writing of books, there is no end (Ecclesiastes 12:12). And where do all these words get us? More books, endless words, heaps of sentences piled on paragraphs, arguments without end.

I think I'll take a nap.

CHAPTER SIX

GREED

My predecessor in Duke Chapel, James Clelland, a Scottish Congregationalist, loved to tell the story that when he was a young preacher he was paid, for preaching a sermon, the then astounding sum of three hundred dollars. On a visit to his dour Calvinist mother in the highlands of Scotland, he proudly told her of his good fortune. Three hundred dollars just for one sermon! Clelland's mother replied, "Oh, son, there used to be a time when to betray our Lord they only had to pay Judas thirty pieces of silver."

Biblical scholars have attempted to ascribe some higher,

theologically more significant motive to Judas's betrayal than the mere thirty pieces of silver. Surely Judas was a Zealot, a would-be revolutionary who was disappointed by Jesus' failure to run out the Romans. Or perhaps Judas was an ambitious conservative who was desperate to court the favor of the Temple authorities.

No, says the Bible, look for no better reason for Judas's betrayal of Jesus than simple Greed. It wasn't the principle of the thing. It was the money. One of the many things wrong with the depiction of Judas in Mel Gibson's film *The Passion of the Christ* is that the Betrayer is depicted as this sinister, possessed, crazed henchman of the devil himself. The Gospels' depiction of Judas is much more realistic, much more believable, much more like us. It wasn't that he betrayed Jesus for some high-flown theological principle. It was the money.

Perhaps that's why it is just a bit easier to lament the evil that is large, systemic, political, natural, and cosmic. Keep sin large, global, universal. Talk about the evil done to us by these wicked institutions, these unjust systems of economic distribution. Jesus might tell us that we don't need to look that far to discover the source of most of the bad that afflicts us.

When Minnesota Senator Paul Wellstone died, someone said at his memorial service that Wellstone always attempted to "temper our Greed." He who would set out to temper our Greed, *my* Greed, will soon be exhausted. Chrysostom's treatise *On the Priesthood* is our most extensive early document on pastoral ethics. It is clear that, when Chrysostom wrote his rules for clergy, he thought that Greed, not Lust, was the chief clerical sin. It's not the genitals; it's the money.

Considered along with some of the other Seven Deadly Sins, Greed is one of those self-evidently bad sins. Charles Dickens, in describing Scrooge, noted the solitary, self-centered nature of Greed. He says of Scrooge, "Oh! But he was a tightfisted hand at the grindstone, Scrooge! A squeezing, wrenching, grasping, scraping, clutching, covetous old sinner! Hard and sharp as flint, from which no steel had ever struck out generous fire; secret, and self-contained, and solitary as an oyster."[1] When Dickens delves into Scrooge's past, we find that his Greed is complex, a mix of childhood cares and adult disappointments. Scrooge was a lonely old man.

Greed tends to be solitary, miserly, because there is something about Greed that puts us in competition with our neighbors and ultimately in alienation from them. In Shakespeare's *Pericles*, fishermen discuss the ways of the world. "Master, I marvel how the fishes live in the sea," says one. Agrees the other, "Why, as men do a-land; the great ones eat up the little ones" (Act 2, Scene 1). There are some sins that hurt only us (Gluttony comes to mind), but *cupiditas* is also a sin against the neighbor.

Buddhism singled out *cupiditas* as one of the three great hurdles of ego-inflation to be conquered on the way to liberation. It is not clear that my consumption of oil is taking petroleum away from the poor of the world. However, it is certainly clear that our consumption is a great contributor to the ecological difficulties in the world. Because I do not know how to extricate myself from the web of complicity that characterizes our consumptive economy, I must pray with particular earnestness, "Lord have mercy upon me, a sinner."

I must labor, in this book, to argue that Sloth or Pride is a sin. I don't have to do that with Greed (despite *Wall Street's* Gordon Gekko's infamous "Greed is good" speech). Who wants to be known as greedy? Yet Greed is a slippery notion. Greed reminds one of our dilemma with Gluttony. We must eat to live. When does normal, healthy mastication get out of hand and become full-fisted gluttony? When does "just making a living" become life with Ebenezer Scrooge? Just as it is difficult to define our basic biological need, our minimum daily requirements for calcium or calories, so it is also difficult to define our minimum daily requirements for art, or music, or attractive clothes. The line between want and need, or desire and necessity, is thin. Human beings are created to be creative, to design and to build, to think and to explore, to add to our world. Things have for us a symbolic function. The church in which I preach is certainly bigger and taller, more finely crafted and elegant than it needs to be in order for us to worship God.

Or is it? We really do need clothing that protects us from the cold, but we also appear really to need clothing that adorns the body and is attractive. Something about us needs a beautiful space in which to praise so beautiful a God. The line between need and desire gets thin.

I certainly do not *need* the computer wherewith I write these words. For nearly two decades I wrote well enough without one; maybe I wrote better, for all I know. I didn't need to give Bill Gates this much money just to enable me to write books.

What am I saying? Of course I need a computer! And a fast one with lots of memory, too. And wireless Internet connections. My life has changed considerably for the better because of this

machine. Just let it go on the blink and you will find me out pac-
ing back and forth in front of my neighborhood computer repair
shop, begging some computer nerd to save my life by fixing this
machine, no matter what it costs.

I have known Christians who take great Pride (yes, that's the
word for it, *Pride*) that they wear old clothes and, even though
they might afford better, drive old cars without air conditioning.
That they make such an effort to live a conspicuously "simple
lifestyle" demonstrates that we human beings are incurably sym-
bol-making creatures who need to adorn ourselves with signs and
symbols that make us human. When does our need for that ever
expanding "more" of life become too much? When does the
desire for the abundant life become the life that is jerked around
by grubby Greed? I expect that you know better when I cross that
line than when you trip over it.

The effort to distinguish between true, absolute need and
merely accidental desire is therefore not as easy as one might
think. Desire—restless, seemingly unquenchable desire—leads us
toward some of the best things that we do. It also leads us into
some of our worst misery. We want more. This is what the economist Say expressed in Say's Law: Demand always rises to meet
supply. The more we have, the more we want.

The psalmist says of the Commandments of God, "More to be
desired are they than gold, even much fine gold . . ." (Psalm
19:10). *Desire* here is the same word that is sometimes rendered
"covet," which means that Greed becomes the only one of the
Seven to make it into the Ten Commandments on the basis of its
link to perverted desire.

Plato urged us to rise above our grubby physical desires, to ascend into that contemplative, ethereal platonic realm where we were no longer slaves to our wants. The noble, philosophical soul is the one who no longer needs all the stuff that makes lesser mortals at least temporarily happy. Nietzsche, then Freud, scoffed at Plato's idealism. Claims that one has at last risen above desire are simple repression of desire rather than extinguishing or redirection of desire, said Freud. Or they are a deflecting of that desire to some other object. It is "sinful" on our campus to desire to drive a forty-thousand-dollar Cadillac but not sinful to drive a used twenty-thousand-dollar Volvo. Desire is crafty.

If there really is no escape from my acquisitive tendencies, why not just give in to them with style? From what I observe, Freud carried the day, at least in the popular imagination. The anything-goes, grab-what-you-can Clinton era was the result. This was followed by the tax-breaks-for-the-rich, massive deficit of the Bush era. "It's your money, keep it," intoned President Bush as millions of Christians voted him in for promised personal prosperity. Enron and Worldcom are us all over. A Bible-believing Baptist, Bernie Ebbers didn't appear to read anything in his Bible, even as an evangelical biblical literalist, that charged him to keep his hands out of the till. We learned to pray the Prayer of Jabez: Lord, increase my holdings!

As Augustine noted, we are afflicted with restless hearts. We want more. Yet our wants are unschooled, wide ranging, free floating, ready to alight on the first sweet-smelling blossom that comes our way. The problem, in the matter of desire, is not that we deeply desire (in fact, apathy, *acedia*, may be a bigger modern temptation than Greed); we desire deeply the wrong things. We attempt to assuage the longing in our restless hearts with that which can never fully satisfy. Buddhism hopes to extinguish some of this raging desire. Christianity hopes to enflame it and to direct it toward its proper object.

We say, "I don't know much about fine food, but I know what I like." Do we? We grab and consume, to a great degree, because we do not really know what we want, and so we grab everything in the desperate fear that we might say no to the one thing that might give our lives some meaning. Advertising feeds on this unfocused, relentless desire, constantly augmenting the objects of our desire, implying that consumption itself is a creative human act, regardless of the objects of our consumption. We exalt our "freedom of choice" as the supreme mark of our freedom when, in our exercise of this freedom, we look like slaves, jerked around by things because we have no means within us of wisely saying yes and no.

The average American spends nearly eighteen hours a week shopping. But that is actually lower than in many other industrialized nations. The philosopher Ludwig Feuerbach famously said something to the effect that "you are what you eat." In other words, what you desire, what you consume, tends to make you. As we consume, we assume that our self is merely acquiring certain articles. But in a curious way, our articles are busy acquiring us. "Clothes make the man." We are all creations of the Gap.

As I visited a parishioner in the hospital after his heart attack, I asked him why on earth he had been burning the candle at both ends, working day and night in his business. He replied, "I was determined to give my little girl the biggest wedding this town ever saw." Is it so wrong that he wanted to be a good parent?

Odd that we should think of Gluttony as the sin that puts us closest to our animalistic desires when it is Greed that best exemplifies matter over mind. At least I think that's what Plato would say. Without the mind restraining, directing, and channeling our desire, we really are the lowest of the primates—none of the apes would have built the Trump Tower. At least none of them would have bragged about it or would have had such success in peddling the multimillion-dollar apartments that enable their inhabitants to look down on everyone else in Manhattan.

The modern capitalist economy encourages us not only to want more but also to want better and to want it faster, which makes our Greed a bit different from that of the ancients. I want more information. And I want it now. One of the skills for surviving, in our society that has so much of so much, is the ability to know when enough is enough, to know when our otherwise admirable desire has led us down the slippery slope of Greed. The New Testament tends to link Greed with idolatry. The first banks were built as temples.

Aquinas says that Greed is a kind of self-delusion, since riches have a way of deceiving us that we can attain self-sufficiency. In other words, Greed becomes a false god, a matter of misdirected worship (Ques. 118, Art. 7). There is a nice fit between our money and our worship of false gods. Thus Exodus parallels the First Commandment—"You shall have no other gods before me" (Exodus 20:3)—with the Tenth Commandment—"You shall not covet your neighbor's house" (Exodus 20:17). God has placed a limit upon our acquisitiveness, recognizing a competitor for our devotion when God sees one.

When they put Jesus to the test, thrusting a coin before him with Caesar's image stamped upon it (Luke 20:24), Jesus surely sought to make this linkage between money and mammon. Where our money is, our heart tends to be (Matthew 6:21).

Our Greed is not only a matter of desire, of wanting something we ought not to want, but perhaps more to the point of idolatry, money is our main means of attaining what we call "security." In Jesus' parable, the Rich Fool attempted to secure his life through money. Alas, you can't take it with you. Psalm 49 mocks the rich because "Mortals cannot abide in their pomp; they are like the animals that perish" (Psalm 49:12). At the rich man's funeral, orators eulogized him for his prudence and careful planning. After the funeral of the rich man with his full barns, God named him "Thou Fool." Now that so much expense and effort and so many lives are being expended in the quest for "national security," I predict that this major motivation for Greed will become even stronger in the years ahead.

If I were making a list of Deadly Sins, Greed would be at the top of my list. Maybe this is just personal, or maybe it is the result of living in this society. We tell the world that we go to war in the Mideast to bring freedom and democracy, whereas much of the world is convinced that it's all about oil. Greed has a way of turning everything that's gold into dross. As James Ogilvy says, "Greed turns love into lust, leisure into sloth, hunger into gluttony, honor into pride, righteous indignation into anger, and admiration into envy. If it weren't for greed, we would suffer fewer of the other vices."[2]

In Greed, our desires get the best of us, bringing out the worst in us. As we have noted, desire is the source of some of the best things that we do. When is it that desire for the goods of this life becomes omnivorous Greed? This is part of the insidious nature of Greed—it can look so much like ourselves at our best. Human creativity, drive, ambition to produce, the desire to leave something of ourselves untouched by the ravages of mortality—all of these otherwise good things can so easily slip into Greed. When does a good thing become too much of a good thing?

Mel Gibson said that he made his movie *The Passion of the Christ* out of his love of God and the church. His film reaped millions, and Gibson made back all of his investment in a couple of days after its Ash Wednesday premiere. Who knows if money was Gibson's major motivation? And if it were, would this negate the good that the film worked among those who saw it and were moved by it? Is it possible for good outcomes to trump bad old Greed?

Perhaps in Greed we are dealing with something like the old "principalities and powers" of the New Testament. That is, otherwise good things gone bad. How can private property, in itself, be evil? The Bible, particularly in the Old Testament, speaks of material possessions as gifts of God, a sign of a life well lived. Yet Christians and Jews have a very peculiar notion of what is "mine": "For all things come from you, and of your own have we given you" (1 Chronicles 29:14). Considering the full sweep of the Christian tradition, one would have to conclude that the most profane word we can utter is that word, *mine*.

Thomas Merton tells of the monk Serapion who sold his Bible

and gave the money to the hungry, saying, "I sold the book that told me to sell all I had and give to the poor. . . ."

Gratitude is sparse in those with Greed, Pride, and Envy, too. Greed is that great lack that enables sin to flourish, that great misreading of the true condition of your situation, that refusal to worship God, the giver of all good gifts. Meister Eckhart said that if the only prayer you ever pray is "thank you," then you have prayed well enough.[3]

I think that a major theological justification for giving to the church and to the poor, for tithing of our income, is as a remedy for Greed. I have found, over the years, that giving away at least ten percent of my income is a way of reclaiming part of what I have as a gift of God, as undeserved, unearned grace. True, ten percent is only a small part of what I have, yet one has to begin somewhere. For me and my house, that ten percent is a sign of our freedom. We may give far too much of ourselves away to acquisitiveness, yet at least there is a percentage of our souls that is, by the grace of God, yet free.

Perhaps Greed comes when good gets out of hand and a virtue overly stressed becomes a vice. When a gift of God becomes "mine," is that where the trouble begins? There is that phenomenon, which many have noted, of the ever-rising threshold of expectation. Stated simply, the more we have, the more we want. We start off wanting to get ourselves over the poverty line, and then it's one thing and another. In this matter of Greed, it is rarely Gordon Gekko's "Greed is good!" Temptation is much more subtle.

When Jesus was tempted in the desert, you will recall that the devil offered him only good things—bread, political power, and miraculous spiritual feats. Once you admit, and I think we must admit, to the goodness of material possessions, then Greed is a very difficult line to draw.

But just because it is difficult, there is no reason why we should not draw such a line. Perhaps we ought to distinguish between what we need and what we want. We need many of the material possessions that we accumulate. We know of the necessity to "meet my needs." Yet how do you meet the ever-expanding reach of desire? Desire has a way of mimicking need. In the marketplace, advertising has a genius for performing that sleight-of-hand that moves us quickly from what we desire to what we need.

We live in a land ruled over by the Constitution that gives us all certain innate "rights." The purpose of this democracy is to give us our rights. Perhaps we are among the first generation in this society to realize that desire has a way of being elevated to the level of need, and need gets further inflated to the level of rights. Our rights are thus an ever-expanding list because my desires are a bottomless pit. Thus noble democracy becomes a relentless commercial supermarket where we rush about grabbing everything we can out of fear that we might neglect the one thing that would give us lives that are worth living.

Need is best if kept close to the basics—a full stomach, a roof over our heads. But it is the nature of desire to be ever growing, ever rising. And where do we get the wherewithal to say no? In our society—with the constant bombardment from advertising (Please, Lord, deliver me from unsolicited e-mail commercials), as well as all of the social affirmation of the "lifestyles of the rich and famous," whom no one dares to call merely Greedy—where might one get the moral stamina to say, "Enough is enough!"?

Perhaps we ought to think of the church as schooling in desire, learning how to want the right things in the right way and the right proportions. Unfortunately, many simply think of the church as just another way to get our needs met. Church is where I get one-stop shopping for the satisfaction of all my spiritual longings and urges. A capitalist economy tends to commodify everything, even Jesus.

The church is not just about "meeting my needs"; the church is also about judging my alleged "need," about giving me needs that I would not have had if I had not met Jesus.

We live in a society that has long since moved beyond the satisfaction of basic human needs to the gratification of all our wants and desires, and the expectation that it is my God-given right to have those wants satisfied. Those who put it politely, by saying that we have moved into a "consumer economy" or a "service economy," are simply noting that those activities and commodities that were once regarded as superfluous and unnecessary have now become the very basis of our economy. In other words, this is a bad neighborhood for those who hope to avoid the sin of Greed.

What we don't need is central economic planning or new laws, more taxes or fewer good-paying jobs. What we need is something much more difficult to get than a Porsche—character. We need the sort of character that is able to look at the world and all it has to offer and at certain key moments say simply, "Thank you, but I'm now satisfied." It takes a huge amount of moral stamina to be able to say, "Yes, we could afford it, but we are not going to buy it, because it does little to contribute to the basic goodness of our lives." We need to switch our economic thinking from the supply side to the desire side of the equation.

It's become downright morally heroic to be the sort of person who could say, "No, thanks. I've already got more than I can possibly consume responsibly." It's become a great parental achievement to say, "Yes, dear, we could afford it, but we love you so much we don't need to buy you that car," or "Trips to Vail to ski every Christmas are fine for Tommy's family but not fine for us. We live by a different story, expect different things of ourselves than Tommy's family."

As we have noted, we are consumers even when it comes to religion. Here, take this, pray that, attend this service, worship here, and you will feel better in the morning. This religious marketing may not be a totally bad thing. Consumers have certain desires and demands, certain expectations for quality, which could be potentially positive for a religious institution. Sometimes uncritical, undemanding congregations get the sermons they deserve!

Unfortunately, the consumer mentality is not a very attractive mental condition. The consumer almost never asks, when consuming, about the larger good. Consumption is mostly about fulfillment of personal desire. Furthermore, consumerism does not mesh well with the gospel. The Christian faith says that church is not about getting what we want but rather about getting what God wants. The Christian faith is God's idea of a good time.

What's so bad about getting "what I want"? One trouble is that

I don't usually know what I want until advertising tells me what I am required to have if I am to live well in this world. Advertising doesn't just meet our needs with its products but creates needs. Advertising manufactures desire. The ads during the Super Bowl are always more interesting than the football game. There would be no game were it not for the ads.

Once, during the middle of a sermon just before the annual orgy of buying that we once called Christmas, I said, "If you bring a young child, say a child of five or six, into this church, the child will be disoriented, will need instruction, will not know what to do next. If you take that same child into Toys "R" Us, no instruction will be required." Then I caught myself in mid-sentence and said, "No, that's not fair to the folk at Toys "R" Us, who have spent millions and utilized some of the best minds that we can produce to instruct this child, through a barrage of ads, that the whole purpose of life is consumption, that life consists in the abundance of their possessions."

None of the Seven Deadly Sins, with the exception of perhaps Lust and maybe even Pride, receives such extensive indoctrination and support from the culture as Greed. Advertising is not simply information; it is also formation. While I might be tempted to say that Greed is quite natural, that we are born with this disposition just as we are born with a propensity to Lust, I wonder if that claim is true. We may be born wanting more, but are we born with such great faith in the goodness of consumption and the blessedness of acquisition?

"Behold, the hand of him who betrays me is upon the table with me," says Jesus to his gathered disciples on that last Thursday supper. As he pronounces this, Jesus cuts his eyes toward Judas. The Son of God comes among us, Word made flesh as our friend, and Judas throws all that away for a fistful of dollars.

Yet Christians take a curious comfort from the presence of Judas there, in the inner circle around Jesus. Nodding in agreement as Jesus speaks of the blessed kingdom of Heaven, smiling sweetly as Jesus talks about the lilies of the field and the birds of the air, there is Judas, ripe for picking by the first person who comes along with some ready cash in exchange for a betraying kiss of the King of Heaven. Satan is said to have "sifted" Simon Peter, leading to his betrayal, and to have "entered" Judas. But did the devil make Judas do it? Our Greed is so close at hand as to seem almost innate. We're glad that Judas was at the table that fateful night because if he had not been, we would be out of place at the table, too.

Thus when Karl Barth, in his massive, revolutionary discussion of the Christian doctrine of Election[4]—God's gracious choice of humanity for redemption—reached for the prime example of the electing grace of God, he chose Judas, money-grabbing Judas. What a great God, said Barth, who would dare to choose Judas to be a disciple, to sit in the inner circle, to perform such a starring role in the redemption of humanity. Judas, the premier disciple. The others betrayed Jesus by scurrying into the darkness like a bunch of frightened rabbits. Judas was an activist, a person who got things done, a courageous go-getter who took matters in hand, went to the authorities, and handed over his best friend to death. He only received thirty pieces of silver for it, but it's the thought that counts.

We pin the deed on Judas, but that's not really the whole story. While at his last supper, Jesus asks all of his disciples, "When I sent you out without a purse, bag, or sandals, did you lack anything?" (Luke 22:35). Earlier Jesus had sent his disciples out, telling them to take nothing with them but to rely only on the goodness of God and their neighbors to survive along the way. He then mentions the need for a sword and they say, "Look, we've got two swords right here" (Luke 22:38, paraphrased). In other words, Jesus says, "When I sent you out and commanded you not to take a bunch of baggage with you, but rather to rely on God alone, did you disobey me?"

The two swords are evidence of their disobedience. The two swords are testimony that, while trust in Jesus and faith in God are fine, just in case, it's good to watch your pension and to carry plenty of insurance. As Jesus says, the whole episode fulfills the Scriptures, "He was counted among the lawless," some of whom happen to be his twelve closest friends.

So once again you and I have reason to be glad that this Son of God "receives sinners and eats with them" (Luke 5:30). Yet Jesus not only receives and befriends sinners; he also calls sinners to repentance (Luke 5:32).

And so our stroll with Greed ends with a question: might I, even I, forego my Greed, my foolish attempt to secure my life through the abundance of my possessions, and learn to live, not by my bank account and pension, but by faith? What a great miracle that would be!

A rich man comes to Jesus, asking him about acquiring some of that eternal life (Luke 18:18ff.)—after all, he has been successful in acquiring so much, why not religion as well? Jesus at first responds by telling him to obey all the Commandments. When the man claims to have done this since his youth, Jesus tells him to sell everything he has, give it to the poor, and come follow him.

I have often wondered if Jesus demanded so much of this rich man, knowing that this would push him over the edge, because this would end any talk about his becoming a disciple. As we have noted, Jesus did not have a particularly soft heart or open hand for the rich.

"How hard it is for those who have riches to enter the kingdom of God!" exclaims Jesus as the rich man walks away.

The disciples speak for us all in asking, "Then who can be saved?"

Jesus responds that, as for the rich, it is more difficult for a rich person to get into the kingdom of God than for a fully loaded camel to get through the eye of a needle. That hard!

Yet then, with a twinkle in his eye, Jesus says, "What is impossible for people is possible with God."

Is it possible that I might learn to put things in perspective, to see the gifted, transitory nature of all my accumulations? It is possible. Yet not possible without transformation, without redemption. Why bother listing these sins without some belief in a Redeemer? In fact, that is surely a source of our widespread avoidance of sin—we no longer believe in a God who forgives, so why on earth admit that we are in desperate need of forgiveness? What good does all of this reflection on sin do us? Not much, unless we have some sense of the possibility of sanctification, some sense that it might be possible, in knowing ourselves better, with God's help, to be better. The purpose of enumerating these Seven is to cultivate virtues. Thus, Adagio says in *Othello* (Act 1, Scene 3), "Virtue! A Fig! Tears in ourselves that we are thus or thus, our bodies are our gardens, to which our wills are gardeners. . . ." It is up to us to cultivate virtue. Yet without a God who seeks the lost, and who saves sinners, a God who can raise the dead and perform miracles, it's all quite impossible. Better simply to say that our sins are human, all too human, unavoidable, and inevitable.

Fortunately, with God all things are possible, even opening the hand of the greedy.

When it comes to combat with the Seven, one must start somewhere. There must be among us who are trying to follow Jesus the cultivation of disciplines and practices that enable us—maybe not a hundred percent of ourselves, but at least some of ourselves—to break free. Because the Seven, like Greed, tend to burrow down so deep in our everyday lives, tend to infect just about everything that we do, one must begin with seemingly small, mundane, daily acts of defiance and resistance. A beginning ought to be made, and one way of attacking Greed where it is most vulnerable is in openhanded gratuitous giving, practice in the arts of letting go.

In the worship of the church, when the offering plate is passed and we are asked to put our money where are hearts are, when we are asked to take a stand, publicly to say just where we are in regard to the things of this world, this may be one of the most radical, countercultural, defiant acts the church demands of us. Thanks be to God that the church does not expect us to engage the Seven on our own, or we would never have any victories against sin, Greed or any other.

CHAPTER SEVEN

GLUTTONY

I n Genesis 2, Eve is said to have been tempted by the serpent because the forbidden fruit "was a delight to the eyes and good for food." Aquinas says that this appealing fruit "was the devil's bait for our first parents."[1] Hunger for food was what got her.

Chaucer gave much weight to this early indiscretion:

O cursed Gluttony, our first distress!
Cause of our first confusion, first temptation,
The very origin of our damnation, . . .

Gluttony has corrupted all the earth.
Adam, and his wife, as well,
From Paradise to labour and to Hell.
Were driven for that vice, they were indeed....

O Gluttony, it is to thee we owe
Our grief! Oh if we knew the maladies
That follow on excess and gluttonies,
Sure we would diet, we would tempt our pleasure
In sitting down at table, show some measure![2]

When Jesus was tempted in the wilderness, it was only after he had fasted for forty days, having nothing to eat, that Satan met him. Hunger was the door whereby the devil entered. "Turn these stones into bread," said the devil. And even though Jesus was famished, he refused. One who could refuse food under such circumstances must be somebody.

Thus was a link forged between food and sin. One of the earliest criticisms of Jesus and his disciples was not that his theology was bad or his biblical interpretation was flawed. Jesus' critics charged, "the disciples of John the Baptist fast, but your disciples eat and drink" (Luke 5:33). In other words, John's disciples abstained. They engaged in religiously based diets. Jesus' disciples were always carousing and eating. They also charged Jesus with being "a gluttonous man and winebibber" (Luke 7:34 KJV). Jesus countered with a string of parables about parties and feasts—the party that was given to welcome home the prodigal son being one of the most famous (Luke 15:11-24).

Anyone reading the Gospel accounts of Jesus' ministry would know why the central act of worship for this faith is a meal; there are so many meals in Scripture. When Jesus ended his ministry with a cup of wine and a loaf of bread in hand, saying that this food stood for everything that he was about, it all seemed to fit. The irony of the Last Supper was that, even as Jesus shared in this convivial meal with his best friends, they were also his most notable betrayers. "The one who has dipped his hand into the bowl with me will betray me," said Jesus (Matthew 26:23). It is striking how even something so warm, grand, and convivial as a meal can be an occasion for sin.

There is no evidence that Jesus was a glutton; that bogus charge was a smear tactic of his critics. Still, for a Savior who talked so much about meals and parties, who featured banquets and feasts in so many of his stories about the kingdom of God, it is odd to find Gluttony in the list of the Seven. Plato, the Buddha, and many others have said many more unflattering things about eating and overeating than Jesus. Plato, with his soul-body dichotomy, had more than a little disgust for the flesh. Christians walk a much more difficult line, with our belief in the Incarnation. Rather than the dualistic view of Plato, we believe that the Word became flesh. True, the Word became flesh, not fat; nevertheless, in any flesh there is usually plenty of fat (now more politely referred to as cellulite).

As expected, dear, moderate Aristotle counseled moderation in eating and drinking. "The man who indulges in every pleasure and abstains from none becomes self-indulgent, while the man who shuns every pleasure as boors do, becomes in a way insensible; temperance is...preserved by the mean."[3] Indeed, I might argue that this was the main difference between the moderation ethics of Aristotle and the celebratory ethics of Jesus—Jesus was big on partying, while the Noble Pagan counseled sober moderation. For contemporary followers of Jesus, it is still somewhat of a scandal that Jesus' first followers were criticized for having too much fun in food and drink. Rarely are the contemporary followers of Jesus so criticized today.

In medieval condemnations against Gluttony, the most beloved text is Romans 16:17-18 (KJV): "Now I beseech you brethren, mark them which cause divisions and offences contrary to the doctrine which ye have learned; and avoid them. For they that are such serve not our Lord Jesus Christ, but their own belly; and by good words and fair speeches deceive the hearts of the simple." A close second is Philippians 3:19: "Their god is the belly." This is shaky scriptural support. Paul appears to have been in a debate about Jewish food laws—should these new Christians, many of whom were Jews, eat kosher or not? For the faithful Jew, every meal is a religious occasion, an event that begins with a blessing, acknowledging food as a gift of God. Therefore to abuse food is to abuse one of God's good gifts.

Gluttony is an odd sin, even without reference to scripture. It has none of the tragic potential of Pride, none of the sinister quality of avarice, nor the potential for righteous indignation that is enjoyed by practitioners of wrath. In her book *Gluttony*, Francine Prose asks, "Who in the world decided that gluttony was a sin? ... Whom exactly does it harm except the glutton himself?"[4] Gluttony is a low, guttural, unimaginative, swine-like sin. I can't think of any great tragic figure in literature who was fat. Comedians are fat; tragedians, never. Shakespeare works hard to make Falstaff tragic—the fat man's fall is mostly comic. Wherever there is Gluttony, there is usually disgust, the terrible morning after the nocturnal binge.

But it is the nature of Gluttony to have its lighter side, and we shall have to work to number it among the Seven. The convivial joys around the table are humanity at our best, and the warm-hearted, generous host who plies us with food and drink is beloved. And then there is the fun of a feast. Some of our very brightest human times are those about the table, and some of our most intimate ties. As we have noted, the sharing of food among friends is the heart of the Christian Eucharist, Holy Communion. When Jesus tells parables that begin, "A man gave a feast and invited his friends..." you know that Jesus is revealing something grand about the kingdom of God.

Why was it, then, that when the first list of chief sins appeared at the end of the fourth century, Gluttony headed the list? Probably because Gluttony was a nice shorthand for all of the "sins of the flesh." Those desert monastics, who compiled the first list of sins, included what tortured them the most—a desire for a good meal. When Gregory the Great finally made his official list, he put Pride at the front and Gluttony was pushed to the back, just one step ahead of its close relative in the flesh, Lust. Gregory probably never missed a meal.

The biblical justification for including Gluttony anywhere on the lists was slim. Chrysostom claimed that it was "Gluttony that turned Adam out of Paradise, gluttony it was that drew down the deluge at the time of Noah." It takes some hermeneutical sleight-of-hand and some swift scriptural footwork to read the story in this way. The fall of all humanity and expulsion from Eden seem an awfully heavy burden to lay on the broad back of Gluttony. The Letter of First Timothy claimed that Greed, not Gluttony, was the "root of all kinds of evil" (1 Timothy 6:10). Before Aquinas could put Pride and Greed at the head of the list, Thomas had to discuss Gluttony at some length in order to justify why he did not put it first.

Paul spoke of the body as the temple of the Holy Spirit, but the context was closer to a discussion of Lust than of Gluttony. In fact, Paul seems to have less condemnation for those who eat too much than for those who are overly scrupulous in their eating, in his discussion of food offered to idols (1 Corinthians 8).

Proverbs 23:20-21 advises not to hang out among drunkards and riotous eaters. And yet Proverbs does not seem to mention overeating, or over-drinking, that often. Ecclesiastes 10:17 warns against over-indulgence, but Ecclesiastes 2:24 says that there is nothing better than that we should eat and drink and enjoy the fruits of our labors. In the Old Testament and the New, feasting is regarded as a sort of summit to human life in this world. The Jewish liturgical year revolved around a succession of feasts. And Isaiah 55 speaks of the Messianic reign, when God would at last set everything to rights, as a banquet where everyone, particularly the poor, would eat their fill.

Tertullian, one of the crabbiest of the Fathers of the Church, manages to explain many of the Hebrews' transgressions in the Old Testament by their inability to control their appetite and their diet. This essentially pagan, Stoic disgust for the body is one of the great theological, unbiblical flaws in many of the Church Fathers' condemnations of Gluttony. The "Golden-Tongued" John Chrysostom uses his tongue rather too excitedly to describe the results of Gluttony: "discharge, phlegm, mucous running from the nose, hiccups, vomiting, and violent belching . . . the increase in luxury is nothing but the increase in excrement."[5]

Augustine, in *On Christian Doctrine*, articulates the conventional view that "in all matters of this kind, it is not the nature of things we use, but our reason for using them, and our manner of seeking them, that make what we do either praiseworthy or blamable."[6] Thus, Augustine's great concern was not what Gluttony did to the body, but what it did to the soul.

Chrysostom, in numerous sermons, condemned those manna-grabbing Exodus Hebrews in the wilderness and named them as our forebears in Gluttony. Aquinas is clear that it is not so much what we put in our mouths, or even how much we put in our mouths, but our inordinate desire for and enjoyment of food that leads us to ruin. It is a God-given right to eat, but to actually enjoy our food, to inordinately enjoy our food, is a sin, said Aquinas. Once again I suspect Aquinas of taking his cues from Aristotle rather than Scripture. Of course, it is rumored that St. Thomas had a rather impressive girth himself.

In Dante's *Inferno*, gluttons find themselves in the third circle of Hell, not the worst of places to spend an eternity but a fate more terrible than that suffered by the lustful. The lustful at least lust after other people. Gluttons sell their souls for roast pig. What I would give right now for a Sam's hotdog with chili and onions is, well, sinful.

Still, why is Gluttony so bad? Augustine asked in his *Confessions* (10.X.31), "Is there anyone, O Lord, who has never incited me on the strict limit of need?" The devil worms in right at the point of need. Eating is essential for the preservation of life. Why make such a big deal of those times when one goes beyond the limits of bodily necessity? We desire and need food even more than sex. In the modern world, where unrestrained Lust is encouraged and its practice thrives, Lust is my candidate for an important sin, despite our rates of obesity. The medievals connected the sins of the mouth with the sins of other orifices of the body, with the mouth leading off.

I find the Church Fathers' linkage of Gluttony and Lust to be interesting. Though I never eat oysters without remembering that scene in the movie *Tom Jones*, it seems to me that that sort of Gluttony could be an impediment to the practice of Lust. (Have you ever seen an R-rated nude scene featuring a 300-pound Romeo?) Saint Basil would disagree. Basil sees a direct link between Gluttony and Lust as "through the sense of touch in tasting—which is always seducing gluttony by swallowing, the body becomes fattened up and titillated by the soft humors bubbling uncontrollably inside, is carried in frenzy toward the touch of sexual intercourse."[7] Wow. That's a more interesting meal than most of us have had.

Saint Thomas says that Gluttony has six daughters and they are named: "Excessive and unseemly joy, loutishness, uncleanness, talkativeness, and an uncomprehending dullness of mind." This seems a fairly severe condemnation of overeating and its possible progeny, but I must say it is no more severe than the condemnations one hears in the fulminations of diet guru Dr. Phil.

Chaucer, in "The Pardoner's Tale," has the pardoner recall the story of Noah, who drank so much that he failed to notice he was sleeping with his own daughters. William Langland's version of *Piers Plowman* condemns those gluttons who "breed like town swine and repose at their ease, till sloth and sleep make slek their sides." And Thomas à Kempis, in *Imitation of Christ*, says, "When the belly is full to bursting with food and drink, debauchery knocks at the door."[8]

Jesus does portray the rich as those for whom food tends to be a spiritual issue. In Luke 16:19, in the story of Lazarus and the rich man, the sumptuous feasting of the rich man was seen as a sign of Greed. The tables are turned in the afterlife. Of course, the teller of this tale is the one who proclaimed, at the beginning of his ministry, "Blessed are you who are hungry now, for you will be filled" (Luke 6:21). Whereas Marie Antoinette said, "Let them eat cake," Mary sang at Jesus' birth about a Savior who would "[fill] the hungry with good things" (Luke 1:53).

The story of Lazarus and the rich man reminds us that Gluttony is more than self-indulgence; it may also be a way of being blind to the needs of others in a world where millions go hungry. Saint Bernard said, "A man can be a glutton over a mess of beans." Augustine taught that a rich man was either a robber or, if he inherited his wealth through the death of his parents, the son of a robber.

In another story of Jesus', it was the rich man who, with stuff-filled barns, said to himself, "Soul, take ease," and thus deluded himself into believing that his surfeit equaled security. Paul, as mentioned previously, writes about the people whose "God is the belly" (Philippians 3:18-19). The gut becomes more important than the soul. The one who was created "in the image of God" exchanges that image for that of the slug and the pig and becomes a mere eating machine. The alimentary canal becomes more important that the brain.

This is all curious, considering that the very summit of Christian worship is a meal, the Eucharist. You are to "taste and see that the Lord is good." Jesus called himself "bread" and told us to "feed on me" (John 6). Can this be a kind of spiritualizing transformation of our tendency toward the sin of Gluttony? In the Eucharist, we are given a very small quantity of food and drink, not enough to engorge ourselves, not enough to assuage our hunger. David Hume argued that "the more men refine upon pleasure, the less they indulge in excesses of any kind; because nothing is more destructive to true pleasure than such excesses."[9] I wonder. Maybe our Gluttony simply becomes more refined, but no less a sin. As for those of us who live in lands that consume most of the world's resources, while much of the world is short on resources, would the rest of the world look upon us as less gluttonous because we are more refined?

Gluttony is sinful just to the degree that some consume too much in a world where others have not enough of the necessities for life. Jesus says, in the story, that the rich man ate in the face of the great need of Lazarus. Lazarus, the man who gladly would have feasted on the crumbs from the rich man's table, was never even noticed by the rich man. In what way does Gluttony constitute an offense against the larger society? Our overconsumption of petroleum and natural resources may be seen as an offense against our neighbor. But attempts by mothers to induce guilt in their children by remembering the starving children of China have not been intellectually compelling.

In Gluttony, it is the excessiveness that is the sin, excessive consumption as well as excessive attentiveness to food. (Perhaps we ought to move our discussion of Gluttony from the matter of food to noise, TV, cars, and the other more notable marks of our conspicuous consumption.) Addiction, bulimia, alcoholism, and the life of the gourmand probably would be classified under the rubric of Gluttony. Beginning with Gregory the Great in the sixth century and on through Aquinas and the Middle Ages, writers understood Gluttony to have five main branches: eating too soon, too much, too avidly, too richly (in the sense of expensively), and too daintily.

To become obsessed with food, to make exaggerated claims for the salutary effects of a good diet, and to build one's whole day around the consumption of food (or, more accurately, controlling and regulating that consumption of food) seems to me the sort of thing that Gregory was after when he condemned eating "too daintily." Gluttony consists in that little word *too*.

Note that Gluttony was not merely wolfing down large quantities of food; Gluttony was also a matter of being overly concerned about food, fixated on food, rather than the amount of food. That person who carefully weighs the "carbs" in her diet—who relentlessly scans the fat content of her portions, who drives across town to buy exclusively "organic"—looks to me as much like the glutton whom Aquinas had in mind as the beer-gutted binger at the neighborhood bar. Refinement can produce its own excess in the priggish food expert. The fat guy in the tee shirt, swilling vast amounts of beer with buffalo wings, is surely no more disgusting than the priggish person, daintily observing, sniffing, and picking over his food. Ought we to be concerned that one of the most widely watched television channels—watched nearly every day by a larger proportion of viewers than nearly every other channel—is the Food Channel? When does concern about good food become too much concern?

C. S. Lewis, in *The Screwtape Letters*, makes this same point: that with Gluttony the problem is not so much the quantity but the quality of our consumption. Screwtape, the devil, notes how the abstemiousness of an old lady is a cover for her self-centeredness:

> But what do quantities matter, provided we can use a human belly and palate, to produce querulousness, impatience, uncharitableness, and self-concern? Glubose has this old woman well in hand. She is a positive terror to hostesses and servants. She is always turning from what has been offered her to say with a demur little sigh and smile, "Oh, please, please...*all* I want is a cup of tea, weak, but not too weak, the teeniest weenniest bit of really crisp toast." You see? Because what she wants is smaller and less costly than what has been set before her, she never recognizes as gluttony her determination to get what she wants, however troublesome it may be to others.

This old lady believes that she is being temperate, when she is being quite demanding.

Why is Gluttony—whether it be taking too much food or taking food too daintily—so great a vice? Wherein the sin? We all must eat to live. If it is a sin, it must be a sin that is very difficult to control, because there is no way to go "cold turkey" and avoid all consumption of food. Therefore John Cassian, the fourth-century monk who helped give birth to the Seven, admitted that of all of them, Gluttony and Lust are illnesses that require "the most creative cures." Because all of us must eat to live, because the ingesting of food is the most natural and necessary of human acts, philosopher David Hume said that to beat up on Gluttony was evidence of the sort of narrow moralism and parsimoniousness for which Hume so gleefully excoriated the Christian faith. Hume said that prudish Christian condemnation of harmless Gluttony said more about the sick character of the one who was doing the condemning than the moral turpitude of the glutton.[10]

Yet, curiously, of all the Seven only Gluttony is today more condemned, feared, and shunned than any of the other sins, though not feared as a sin. For most of us, the repulsive thing that gets us about Gluttony is not the sin but the fat, that globulous bane of middle-aged existence, that to which Americans are succumbing in alarming numbers. Gluttony is an outrage against our ideal body image, not infidelity against God. For most of us, any "sin" in Gluttony is in the resulting ugliness and possibly ill health, but mostly ugliness. Therefore, if we would consider the perils of overeating, the discussion ought to be around matters of aesthetic beauty, not moral good.

Little there is in the Christian faith that makes ugliness a matter of sin; the pressure to make obesity a sin comes from American culture. A recent study shows that eleven percent of Americans would abort a fetus if they were told that that fetus had a tendency toward obesity. Elementary school children say that they are more judgmental toward the fat kid in class than they are toward a bully. Studies have shown that an overweight person is at a distinct disadvantage in being hired for a job when compared with someone who is not overweight. Although excessive fat can be due to a variety of factors, most of us, whether we openly admit it or not, ascribe obesity to laziness, lack of self-control, or emotional problems. There is a curious schizophrenic tendency in our contemporary approaches to Gluttony. On the one hand, we live in a culture of self-indulgence with a "Be good to yourself!" philosophy. On the other hand, when it comes to food, we are stricken with deep pangs of conscience, guilt, and remorse. Even the corpulent Dr. Johnson said, "It is the just doom of laziness and gluttony to be inactive without ease, and drowsy without tranquility." We have demonized gluttons in ways that we would not think of doing with the other sins.

Perhaps our contemporary condemnation is because the effects of Gluttony are remarkably external. The sinner who commits Lust can go about his or her way secretively forever and never be found out. But the glutton is exposed for all to see. That we are so careful to avoid the sin of Gluttony certainly suggests that we are much more concerned with externals than internals, that we care more about the state of our waistline than the state of our souls. We may have deconsecrated Gluttony, but it is still regarded as a serious "sin." Just check out the vast dieting section of your local bookstore.

The representative of my neighborhood gym was trying to convince me to plunk down $300 for a yearly membership in his club for the wannabe ex-plump. It seemed a high price to pay for sweat. But I noticed a huge blob of yellowish, rather disgusting, rubbery, plastic material sitting on the edge of his desk. I asked him what that could possibly be. He picked it up, threw it from one hand to the other, and said, "Mr. Willimon, this is what five pounds of your fat looks like. For $300, we can rid you of this disgusting burden." I paid the money.

Though Dante put gluttons in the third circle of Hell, where they wallowed in the mud like hogs, severe condemnation of fatness is a fairly recent phenomenon. When the poor were all thin, fatness was a virtue, sign of divine favor, mark of nobility. The women of Rubens certainly have no problem with their portliness. Today, in North America, the poor are found disproportionately among the ranks of the obese, and thus there is an economic dimension to our cult of thinness. Though there is nothing to suggest that all fat people are gluttons, or poor, when we look at a fat person, we suspect that they are guilty of Sloth and Gluttony, until proved otherwise. Don't you find it curious that, even in our allegedly permissive, nonjudgmental society, Gluttony is the one of the Seven that today tends to be more severely, universally condemned than any of the others? What's a little Lust among friends, and Pride can be, as we have noted, downright attractive, but Gluttony? Unforgivable.

Perhaps the obesity of the poor deserves our sympathy rather than our condemnation. Aquinas graciously excuses an ignorant or uninformed person from condemnation for the sin of overindulgence: "A man is excused from sin when he is not aware of the strength of the drink, and also when he does not know the weakness of the man he invites to join him. There is no excuse in either case unless ignorance is present." He also quotes Augustine, who says that, when it comes to the excesses of feasting and carousing, "such things are not to be banished with bitterness, harshness, and high-handedness, but rather by instructing than commanding, by advising not threatening. Such is the course to be followed with most sinners; few are they whose sins are to be visited with severity."[11] Agreeing with these saints,

I have therefore tried to banish some of the Seven with a lighter, rather than a heavier, hand.

Can you tell?

Gluttony was always considered to be a close friend to Sloth. This seems right to me, for medieval Sloth was more than simple laziness. As we have noted, Sloth was the sense that one was excluded from the forgiving and embracing grace of God, that one had no vocation, that is, from our point of view, a brand of extremely low self-esteem that feeds (literally) on whatever it can get to take away some of the pain of exclusion. We all know that overeating can be related to a sense of emptiness within. Binge eaters today seem to be filling the void that is much deeper than their stomachs.

I would quite willingly link Gluttony to Pride. In medieval times, feasts were conspicuous displays of one's riches. Today, to be able to brag about having a two-hundred-dollar dinner at a restaurant could be an occasion for Pride, and possibly linked to Greed. Once, when invited by a man to a ten-course, four-hour marathon dinner of Asian food flown into Durham, I asked my host, between the thousand-year-old eggs and the Peking duck, "Do you always eat like this in your culture?"

He replied, "I have seen starvation. Mao starved to death most of the people in my village, among the millions who starved to death in the early days of the Communists."

That sort of explained it all. Our North American culture has made few truly original contributions to the development of the human race, but surely one of them is the diet. The Seven are ancient inclinations, and we have in the modern age made few original contributions to their practice. However, when it comes to Gluttony, our age is uniquely related to this sin. No other age, and no other culture, puts such stress on abstemiousness, is so ruthless in its condemnation of this weakness. Maybe no other culture had enough food to worry about overeating. Don't you find it odd that in our uniquely self-indulgent age, we spend so many millions attempting to encourage abstinence and self-control in this one area of indulgence?

One-third of all Americans, approximately 63 million, are overweight. Fifteen percent of American children are overweight. Two hundred and fifty thousand deaths are attributable to poor diet and inactivity. Fifty percent of cardiovascular disease is related to excess weight. We spend as much as $50 billion a year dieting. Laparoscopic gastric bypass surgery has become the new status surgery for the rich, more chic than a face-lift. That $50 billion for diets is more than we spend on education, training, employment, and social services. We spend more on dieting than the gross national product of Ireland.[12]

Gluttony has become a sickness, as have many of the Seven, a psychological problem, something that is laid on you by your mother, who pushed homemade cake at you in an inept attempt to show you love, a curse under which you labor due to psychological, genetic, hormonal, or environmental factors.

On the other hand, Gluttony is viewed as something that you can actually do something about. Indeed, you have a sacred responsibility to step up to the challenge and shed those ugly pounds.

We waver between believing that we are trapped in fat, by

forces that are totally out of our control, and believing that we are very guilty and very bad if we don't rise up out of our weakness and summon forth the courage we need to control our lives. We are either victims or gods when it comes to Gluttony.

And, if you don't think that you are prejudiced against overweight people, Francine Prose says just check out your feelings when you settle into an airplane seat next to an overweight person who spills over into your space. Studies have shown that grossly overweight people have more difficulty getting mortgages and that people are more apt to think that overweight people are "lazy" or "have poor self-discipline." Recently, says Prose, an obese child was taken away from its parents, and its parents were convicted of child abuse and neglect because of their child's weight. How curious that of the Seven Deadly Sins, few are still regarded as "sins," Gluttony being the one exception.

It is ironic that eating, a necessity for the life of the body, when indulged in the wrong way, becomes detrimental to the body. Gluttony, being normal, necessary ingestion gotten out of hand, has an unavoidability about it. When do we cross the line? When does normal eating and concern for diet become "too much, too little, too daintily" gluttonizing? Yet isn't this just the sort of irony that is inherent in so much of our sin? Life's necessities, when abused, become life's threat.

I suppose it is this biological argument—the detriment that Gluttony proposes for the body—that is our major case against Gluttony, now that we are no longer so concerned with sin. For the medieval moralists, such concerns were relatively unimportant. For them, it was what Gluttony did to the soul that bothered them. Furthermore, medieval theologians give one the impression that Gluttony and Lust are most sinful if we allow ourselves to *enjoy* these activities. Sex engaged in for procreation is smiled upon. Eating that is done for survival is morally neutral. The more negative side of Christian asceticism rears it ugly head. Thus when Gregory the Great condemns Gluttony, he condemns it as "the mother of lust" that eventuates in "groaning of the bowels, . . . of lust, pollution of the intellect, weakness of the body, difficult sleep, gloomy death."[13] In our day, we have no such misgivings about the goodness of pleasure and our right to enjoy whatever we please. What we want is pleasure that does not unduly harm us. "Safe Sex." "Sensible drinking." Low-fat devil's food cookies.

Historically, gluttony was not a particularly terrible sin—perhaps the economic conditions in the Middle Ages kept it from being so. It was only one of the Seven. Curiously, in our day, it appears to have become the worst of sins. As Francine Prose sees it, gluttons are viewed as the brunt of jokes; they are regarded as "freaks or sociopaths, or, even more commonly as ordinary losers, misfits, unfortunate human specimens."[14] Aquinas, more gracious than Dr. Phil, says that "the commoner the sin the less disgraceful it is, and the less shame-making." The intemperance of Gluttony is one such common sin: "Its occasions come into the ordinary run of life, where many of us go wrong. Consequently sins of intemperance are not such a disgrace."[15]

Perhaps Gluttony is a particular problem in a society of instant gratification, where we pursue cheap thrills, where we want momentary satisfaction. I remember the columnist William

Rasberry giving a lecture on "the most detrimental point in human history." What was the worst invention, that which led to the downfall of the human race? Rasberry said it was when humanity learned to refine sugar!

Earlier, when humanity wanted to satisfy its cravings for sweetness, it had to wait until it found some honey or until fruit ripened. Now, with refined sugar, we could have sweetness anytime we wanted. A genetically induced craving could be satisfied instantly, without delay or cost. This, said Rasberry, led to drug addiction, overeating, and a host of other problems. It's an awful lot to claim for granulated sugar; still, there is no doubt that ready availability of food, without any economic restraints upon consumption, aggravates Gluttony.

One reason why we preachers do not have to focus much on Gluttony is that the new moralists related to Gluttony are the doctor, the personal trainer, the aerobics instructor, and the pill-pusher. We flatter ourselves in thinking that we are a sex-obsessed culture. Food is really our cultural downfall and obsession.

I work at a university where a large proportion of women undergraduates suffer, at one time or another, from eating disorders. Eating disorders are thought by us to be an illness rather than a sin. And yet, as an illness, eating disorders have moral dimensions, considering all the moralizing that goes on about our overeating. Our moral censure is reserved for those whose eating disorders make them too fat, rather than too thin. We tend to feel compassion for those whose abuse of eating makes them too thin, and yet we feel condemnation for those whose abuse of eating makes them too fat. Go figure.

I expect that what we call bulimia and anorexia both qualify for what the Christian moralists called Gluttony. Were they merely wrong in this? Anytime we make the belly a god (Philippians 3:19) and obsess over it, worrying about it too much positively or negatively, this would be considered Gluttony, not only as self-abuse but also as abuse of our relationship with God. While fasting was an approved Christian discipline, excessive fasting was condemned as a sign of sin in body and soul. The Christian moralists knew that the compulsive and aggressive faster could be guilty of the sin of Pride. The problem with too much food, or too great a concern about food, is that little word *too*. Fat today tends to be the curse of the lower class, while anorexia tends to afflict the upper class. Gluttony in service of Pride, also abstemiousness in service of Pride, can have sad consequences.

Repentance and remorse, once related to all sin, now seem to accompany only Gluttony. It is not only the morning-after syndrome, but also the proudly displayed photographs of "before" and "after." "Look! This is me, as a size fifty-eight." True dramatic turnarounds from Gluttony appear to be comparatively rare, as low as twenty percent if one counts those who stay on the wagon after their diet. But the stories of truly reformed gluttons are celebrated by Dr. Phil and Oprah. Fat, and what to do about it, is the second largest industry in my town, Durham, North Carolina, the "Diet Capital of the World."

Disgust is our only means of keeping Gluttony at bay. I am not sure how high on the moral scale is disgust, as virtue, but disgust is about as much as we can muster against Gluttony. To take Gluttony seriously, as a serious sin, as an inclination that is worthy of the name "sin" rather than merely a sickness, is to judge our contemporary notions of evil. It is just a bit easier to lament the evil that is large, systemic, political, natural, and cosmic than to admit that it is personal, a matter of the gut. Keep sin large, global, universal. Talk about the evil done to us by these wicked institutions, these unjust systems of economic distribution.

Jesus might tell us that we don't need to look that far to discover the source of most of the bad that afflicts us. We are full of hungers that we attempt to assuage in ways that bring us, our neighbor, and God to grief. We are, by our nature, sinners.

Our sin is linked to who we are as persons. Perhaps that is why Chaucer, Dante, and Spenser, all gifted Renaissance writers, personified the Seven Deadly Sins. They depicted the sins as embodied in different personality types. Of course Gluttony was the fat, middle-aged man who looks suspiciously like me as I stand upon the bathroom scales in the morning. Envy was a sickly woman with yellowish skin. They thus turned the Seven Deadly Sins from ideas or abstract concepts into people like us, people like me. We look in the mirror and see the Seven Deadly Sins staring us back in the face. Sin is not some alien force, some demonic possession. Sin looks like me.

CHAPTER EIGHT

LUST

From time to time (not as often as I would like) some student asks me about sex in the Bible: "What does the Bible say about sex before marriage?" or "What does the Bible say about sexual orientation?" Stuff like that. Then I'm forced to answer, "Well, next to nothing." Certainly, less is said in the Bible about sexual sin than is said by my church. One thing unites theological conservatives and theological liberals these days: they both believe that sex is an awfully important subject for Christians.

Earlier I have admitted that there is scant biblical justification for some of the Seven Deadly Sins. Here, when it comes to Lust, we must admit it again. There's just not much good scripture on Lust. A few years ago, when *The DaVinci Code* was all the rage, after an evening's discussion of the book with students I said, "I don't think this book tells us anything about Jesus, but it tells us a lot about us." That we should have such curiosity about the sexuality of Jesus, his possible romantic attachments, Mary Magdalene as a girlfriend, and so on, is telling. We can't imagine a human being who is not obsessed with sex. We cannot follow a Savior for whom sexuality was not a major, defining concern.

Despite popular wisdom, Christianity is notoriously lax with "sins of the flesh," the habitat of Lust. As C. S. Lewis puts it in *Mere Christianity,*

> The sins of the flesh are bad, but they are the least bad of all sins. All the worst sins are spiritual: the pleasure of putting other people in the wrong, of bossing and patronizing and backbiting; the pleasures of power, of hatred. For there are two things inside me, competing with the human self which I must try to become. They are the Animal self, and the Diabolical self. The Diabolical self is worse.[1]

Lust is one of the least creative of the Seven. In Lust, our so-called lower nature comes to the fore, much as it does in Gluttony. Dogs do coitus as well as humans, maybe better, for all I know. It takes a human brain to do Envy, and the hoarding instinct that we find in the animals is something quite less than the summits, or depths, of human Greed. But Lust is that sin that requires not a brain, but rather the action of the other "less honorable" (as Paul would delicately put it) organs of the body.

Shakespeare is tougher on Lust than Paul is. His father's ghost says to Hamlet, "So lust, thought to a radiant angel link'd, will sate itself in a celestial bed, and prey on garbage" (*Hamlet*, Act 1, Scene 5). And then there's that wonderful, repulsive, disdainful Shakespearean sonnet on Lust:

> The expense of spirit in a waste of shame
> Is lust in action; and till action, lust
> Is perjured, murderous, bloody, full of blame,
> Savage, extreme, rude, cruel, not to trust,
> Enjoy'd no sooner but despised straight,
> Past reason hunted, and no sooner had
> Past reason hated, as a swallow'd bait
> On purpose laid to make the taker mad;
> Mad in pursuit and in possession so;
> Had, having, and it quest to have, extreme;
> A bliss in proof, and proved, a very woe;
> Before, a joy proposed; behind, a dream.
> All this the world well knows; yet none knows well
> To shun the heaven that leads men to this hell.
> (*Sonnet 129*)

Somehow that sonnet made more sense to me when I first heard it as a college sophomore than now. What the spirit can't cure in our lustful proclivities, deteriorating flesh usually handles. Lust is an ancient malady, but one could argue that technology enables this sin to be worse for us. I read that the greatest growth in "e-commerce" is porn. The Web is peculiarly well-suited for the exercise of, and encouragement of, Lust, which tends to be one of the most secretive of the Seven. Even in my own limited experience, I can name you half a dozen clergy who have been removed from the Christian ministry because of their engagement with pornography on the Internet.

Lust has a kinship linguistically with a host of words that crop up in the writings of the Fathers, all of them pejorative: *luxuria*, rankness, luxuriance; *luxo*, to put out of place, out of joint (Greek, *loxos*, slanting, oblique); *luxor*, to riot, revel, live luxuriously; *luxum*, a dislocation; *luxus*, debauchery.[2] Which makes it all the more strange that Lust, along with Pride, has undergone considerable rehabilitation in our own day. None of us wants to be accused of Envy or Greed, but Lust has become a quite endearing characteristic of modern enlightened folk like us. In modern life, the only damaging thing about Lust is suppressing it. "Deny thyself" is not a watchword of our age. Who wants to be labeled a prude? Our slogan is that of Mae West: "When I'm good, I'm very, very good, but when I'm bad, I'm better."[3]

In an earlier day, masturbation was a sin. Now, it's a cure.

So if we think of Lust as a sin at all, we probably consider it an ambiguous sin, "human, all too human." The fruits of Lust—sexual assault, domestic violence, the abuse of children—can be terrible, among the most universally condemned and severely punished of crimes. But who knows of a human who has never committed Lust? In a notoriously difficult statement Jesus said, "You have heard that it was said, 'You shall not commit adultery.' But I say to you that everyone who looks at a woman with lust has already committed adultery with her in his heart" (Matthew 5:27-28). I don't know why Jesus didn't include women in that injunction, but, well, if even to think Lust is to lust, then who among us is free of this sin? I once had a psychotherapist tell me that she could never be a Christian because of Jesus' ridiculous denunciation of "lust in the heart." She said that she had treated so many hung-up, conflicted, sadly repressed, and guilt-ridden people whose lives had been damaged by that statement. I told her that she must be treating a population other than those in my church. My people are more likely to feel guilt that their lives are not completely consumed with sex rather than that they are committing "lust in the heart" or at any other anatomical location. In a sex-saturated, sex-infatuated culture, the words of Jesus on Lust will seem awfully overwrought. Why make such a big deal over something so prevalent and widely practiced and praised as Lust?

Lust, like so many of the Seven, presents us with a paradox. How odd that sexuality, presented in Genesis 1 as a gift of God, is by the second creation story of Genesis 2 presented as a curse. In the first creation story sex is a means of humanity sharing in some of God's own fecund creativity and generativity (Genesis 1:26-28). By the second creation story sex is presented more ambiguously. In that story, woman is created from the "rib" of man and is therefore subordinate, derivative (Genesis 2:22). The woman is called the "help-mate" of man (Genesis 2:18), which again implies a kind of subordination, rather than equality. True, by the end of the story (Genesis 2:24-25), man and woman are linked in solidarity in sin, for both are equally disobedient.

By the very end of the creation story, when the primal woman and man are excluded from God's good garden, the man and the woman are clearly at odds with each other. Childbirth, a creative blessing of God, will be also a cause of great pain. The woman will "desire" the man, and the man "shall rule over" the woman. This is clearly not the state of the world as God created it to be, but rather as our sin and rebellion have made it. God created us for mutuality, and the mutual sharing of sexuality, yet our disordered state has made even sex a curse, a war between the sexes, a means of one gender idolatrously lording over another. Things were fine in the Garden until we got there with our curiosity and our desire, our omnivorous desire. "It was not the apple on the tree but the pair on the ground that caused the problem in the garden," said M. D. O'Connor.[4] It was not "the devil made me do it." We are quite capable of rebelling against God without any supernatural prompting.

The sin in so many of the Seven is in our perversion of the good, and with Lust it's no different. The unabashed, innocent, mutual eroticism of the youthful Song of Solomon is sex as it is meant to be. The sad, deadly results of King David's Lust for Bathsheba is sex as we have made it. How could it be that such a good, godly gift like sex could be, in our hands, such a sorrow?

Well, that's always the way it is with our sin, right? Dante said that sin is love gotten badly out of fix. The Seven are loves perverted, loves attached to the wrong objects, for the wrong reasons, and in the wrong ways. Thus Dante felt that the perpetrators of the Seven belong in temporary purgatory rather than in the eternal torment of Hell. Those who succumb to the sins of the flesh such as Lust (and who does not?) are more confused than perverse. Desire is a good, God-given thing. Desire misdirected, misused, leads to sin.

Aquinas admits that Lust is a big problem because, in his words, "it is congenial to our nature." What a marvelous apostolic understatement. Walk out of here and wander into the world just a few minutes, mix it up in human society for only a short time, and try, really try to obey Jesus' injunction against "looking at another person lustfully." You'll learn that, for all your virtues, you are a certified sinner. Lust is indeed "congenial to our nature."

(By the way, Aquinas notes that there is something about the sin of Lust, particularly in others, that seems to attract perverse Christian moral curiosity. Therefore be suspicious of my moral outrage against Duke sophomores for their promiscuity. In one week Congress spent more energy debating the outrage of Janet Jackson's exposure at the Super Bowl than it did debating the morality of the then current war with Iraq. While inquisitiveness toward the sins of others can be edifying as "an encouragement to do better," Aquinas warns that "to pry and dwell on our neighbour's faults in order to despise him ... is vicious."[5])

In *The City of God* Augustine has a passage in which he, attempting to make the point that our wills are weak and ineffectual, points to the male member as an example (something I would never use as a sermon illustration). Augustine notes that the male sexual organ is limp when it ought to be firm, and firm at the most inopportune times when it should be limp. Augustine mockingly reasons that if we cannot even control such an inferior organ of the body through our determination, decision, and will, what makes us think that we can control our souls? He moves from there to a discussion of the limits of free will and the sovereign action of God's grace in our salvation.

Sorry, if you thought church was a place where we come to work at avoiding sin. Church is where we come to name our sin. (Oscar Wilde quipped, "If your sins find you out, why worry! It is when they find you in, that trouble begins."[6]) We are, good old Lust charges and convicts us, sinners. We live in a paradoxical caughtness. God has given us good gifts like sex that enable us to participate in some of the divine creativity, and we abuse and misuse those gifts. We make all sorts of high-sounding determinations not to sin, not to think certain thoughts, not to have roving eyes, and yet we do.

Just as the gospel begins with the temptation of Jesus in the wilderness and his resistance to those temptations, so our temptations reveal both who we are and what we might become. Thomas à Kempis writes, "Fire proveth iron, and temptation a just man. We know not oftentimes what we are able to do, but temptation showeth us what we are" (*Imitation of Christ*, I, 13). This suggests that the person who has never really felt the tug of temptation has never really lived, has never desired anything of worth, has no idea who he or she really is. For my money, nothing so well demonstrates our weaknesses, our identity, down deep, as sinners, as does good old Lust.

Meister Eckhart, master of irony, is so bold as to say, "Betimes it is the will of God that I commit sin."[7] God has put in us desire, and sometimes that desire becomes the very source of our worst sin. And sometimes that succumbing to sin is revelation of who we really are and how badly we need a God who saves sinners.

Fortunately, the gospel is not just a declaration that we are all sinners. The gospel is also a statement that Jesus Christ died for sinners. Only sinners. Our sin is what nailed him to the cross, our big and little slipups, screwups, even our doggy-like sins like Lust. Yet (now, the good news) as Paul put it: "Where sin increased, grace abounded all the more" (Romans 5:20).

The Fathers are clear that Lust is not only sexual. There can be all sorts of Lust. We say that we are "just dying" for a piece of candy. We see our neighbor in a new Lexus and passion rises within us for the same car.

I wonder if in our culture there is so much sexual passion and so little desire for God because sex has become the last means of self-transcendence. Sexual passion is our last means of getting outside ourselves, of having ourselves caught up in something greater than ourselves, our last momentary experience of mystery, our sole sacrament. It is not too great an overstatement to say that my job as a preacher is to make discipleship as interesting as orgasm.

We ask of sex something that it can't deliver. I think of this often during a movie when the movie does a good job of getting some difficult, painful human problem out on the table for consideration—such as the life worth living, or the marriage worth having—and then ends in a romp between the sheets, as if sex were the cure for every ailment. What on earth does that have to do with anything? I ask myself at these movies. You may feel better for a moment, but you are still you, your life is unchanged, and you are still stuck where you were. Whoever said, "Love is the answer," could not have been talking about sexual love, which, no matter how momentarily good it gets, is not good enough fundamentally to change us. That's part of the fun of sex; it is so momentary, transitory, and fleeting. We thus confuse a temporary, momentary experience with a long-term solution, a short-lived experience of mystery with an experience of the true and living God, and that's the sin.

Can we do any better? The trouble with pointing out that some of the Seven like Lust are perfectly natural, virtually unavoidable, human-all-too-human inclinations is that we despair (*acedia!*), throw up our hands, throw in the towel, and stop trying to be better. But God has created us not for sin but for salvation. We have been created for eternal communion with God and our hearts are restless to engage in true love rather than love's pale substitutes. Jesus died to justify sinners to God, but he also died and lived, taught and acted, in order to sanctify sinners for God.

I remember a seminarian who came to me deeply troubled by his proclivity to Lust. He confessed that he was guilty of downloading pornography on the Web. At first I was easy with his sin. I reminded him that he was, after all, twenty-three, that God had made people his age for marriage. However, in order to be in graduate school, he had deferred matrimony and was living a lonely, monkish existence, so his desire was quite understandable. While pornography was not a good thing, I could understand how a young man might be attracted to pornography due to his unfulfilled desires.

"But I really want to do better," he protested. "I think that God cares about my thoughts and my actions. I'm really trying to follow Jesus and I don't want any part of my life to be isolated from discipleship."

I was wrong; he was right. We are called not only to name and to confess our sin but also to be free of our sin. By the grace of God we can get better. The Christian faith claims not only that we can be honest about our Lust but also that we can be free of our Lust. We can be free, not only by focusing our thoughts and desires on higher things, not only by having Jesus transform our practice of "love" into all that God means it to be, but also through discipline. There is great interest now in "spiritual disciplines," something we had not heard much about for a long time.

I'll also make a very Wesleyan statement: sometimes I wonder if the church called Lust a deadly sin because, in its wisdom, the church knew that there was just about no sin more difficult to banish from our thoughts *by ourselves*. Condemnation of Lust, insistence that we ought to be free of Lust, was a nice way of reminding us that no one was ever meant to follow Jesus in solo. Christian discipleship is too demanding to go it alone. We need help from our friends. We must not only want to do better but also have specific, orderly, methodical steps to do better. We must get ourselves into a group than enables us to be better than we could be on our own.

A student was telling me about his "holiness group." A group of four to six students meets and covenants together to follow a few disciplines each day. In this group their list was: pray at the same time each day for members in the group, by name; be careful in your language to avoid gossip and cursing; read the Bible at the same time every day; practice sexual chastity; meet weekly to confront one another about your mutual spiritual growth; and confess your sins to one another. I found all this rather amazing. In a chaotic, unstable moral environment— such as the modern university campus—I think it's great that these young Christians are not only naming their sins but also wrestling with their sins.

Christian thought against the Seven Sins can imply a seemingly heroic view of the moral life. Who on earth is a good enough individual to resist such perfectly natural human inclinations? Well that's just the point. No one as *an individual* can resist sin. God does not expect heroic individualism from us but rather membership in a family, a new people, a holy nation called Israel and Church. As lonely, weak, and detached individuals we are no match for the wiles of the Devil. In a group that confirms our struggle to be disciples, we can be so much more than we could have been if left to our own devices. The ultimate "remedy for sin" from a Christian point of view is not tight-fisted moral determination to be better or a cold shower to cool our passions, but is rather baptism by which we are placed in a family that enables us, even us, to be holy.

Reining in Lust is particularly tough in a society that inculcates in us the notion that expression of desire is a right, a duty for each of us, and that the only danger is repression of desire rather than its expression. In a capitalist economy, the government no longer refers to us as "citizens" but rather as "consumers." One way of thinking of even something so noble as higher education is to see it as expensive, subtle training in the arts of unlimited desire and consumption. In a world of untutored, unbridled desire, we tend to grab at everything out of the fear that we might neglect to seize the one thing that would give our lives meaning. Thus the lines between Greed, Envy, and Lust become blurred. The desert Fathers noted that sin tends to feed upon sin. In my town at least, the very worst domestic murders are committed because of Lust. The tendency of Lust to breed violence is a rebuke to any who would dismiss it as harmless. The

Fathers also taught that every time we succumb to one of these tendencies, that tendency is strengthened within us. Sin breeds upon sin. The most important step in resisting Lust is thus the very first, that first baptismal step when we say, "God has created me for more. I say no!"

Take that as a definition, at least in this particular context, of a disciple. A disciple of Christ is someone who, by the grace of God, has somehow been given the ethical resources to be able to look upon all the wiles of the world and say no.

Years ago, Tom Wolfe wrote an essay on pornography. He quoted Larry Flynt as saying that his pornography performed a public service. People with dark sexual thoughts could respond to those thoughts by merely looking at a pornographic magazine. This kept them from ever acting on those thoughts by committing rape or sexual abuse. The pornography acted as a kind of pressure valve on a steam boiler. Pornography let off some of this steam in a harmless way that kept the person from exploding.

Wolfe countered that the brain is more of a computer than a steam boiler. Garbage in, garbage out. Perhaps the pornography is encouragement to sin, rather than a harmless release of sinful tendencies.

Aquinas sees "simple fornication" as a violation of Jesus' demand for us to love our neighbor. Aquinas looks beyond the coitus toward the child who is produced by our trysting. He says, "Simple fornication is contrary to the love we should bear our neighbour, for, as we have indicated, it is an act of generation performed in a setting disadvantageous to the good of the child to be born."[8] I think it is quite typical of Christianity at its best to worry about the effects of our sin upon others, particularly the smallest, weakest, and most vulnerable of our neighbors. When modern birth control (Note that that's what we call it: *control*. That's what we want, control. "Ye shall be like gods," all over again.) disjoined coitus from conception, sexuality from responsibility to children, it was one of modernity's saddest moments.

Aquinas puts forth the notion that, when it comes to sex, it's the thought that counts. He first says "Kisses, embraces, and caresses signify no mortal sin. They can be done without libidinousness according to the custom of the country or from some fair need or reasonable causes." But even in an act so serious as fornication, "consent to its pleasure is to be gravely wrong. Consequently when kisses and embraces and so forth are for the sake of this pleasure they are mortal sins. Then only are they called libidinous, and to be treated as mortal sin."[9] The key to the sin in sex is in the pleasure, says Aquinas.

Again, Thomas says that "lechery consists . . . in a person applying himself to sex pleasure not according to right reason. This may come about either because of the nature of the act in which pleasure is sought or, when this is rightful, because, some due conditions are not observed."[10] Now this stricture against sex for pleasure may seem quite strange to us who live in a culture where sex has no meaning other than personal pleasure. Isn't Aquinas being terribly (typically?) dour and stuff-shirted in his warning about sex for pleasure alone?

Perhaps we Christians overlook how countercultural it is for the church to assert that all of life, even our sexual life, is to be lived for the glory of God and the good of the neighbor. In losing the sense that our lives are created and owned by God, we have lost any real sense of vocation, any real awareness of our lives being claimed and commandeered by God for any good outside our lives. For Christians to say that the proper, ultimate end of sexuality is children rather than momentary personal pleasure is a radical, subversive claim against the culture of hedonistic nihilism. All good sex, for Christians, is meant to be public rather than private—that is, it is meant to be judged by its contribution to the good of the larger society.

Martin Marty took the prayers of confession in the *Book of Common Prayer* and the Roman Catholic Act of Contrition and compared them with some recent "confessions" by prominent sinners and showed the great gap between our notions of sin and the church's classical teaching. His list really highlights the distinctiveness of Christian sin. He called the article "Kinda Sorry."

We have erred.

"I didn't think I'd get caught."—Baseball star Pete Rose, after he was charged with outlawed sports gambling

We have strayed from Thy ways like lost sheep.

"I sincerely regret my actions in this case."—The *USA Today* executive who embezzled $3.6 million

We have followed too much the devices and desires of our own hearts.

"I am...just a man who made a terrible mistake."—Illinois child pornographer convicted of sex acts against a little neighbor girl

We have offended against the holy laws.

"I'm sure that I'm supposed to act all sorry or sad or guilty."—Rose

We have left undone those things which we ought to have done.

"I was wrong in failing to truthfully address these issues."—Connecticut Governor John Rowland, after misusing state accounts and lying about it

And there is no health in us.

"Give Mr. Rowland credit for at least saying he's sorry."—*Wall Street Journal* editorial

We have done those things which we ought not have done.

"If anyone was offended, I apologize."—California Governor Arnold Schwarzenegger, accused of groping women

I detest all my sins.

"I apologize to anyone I might have offended."—Fuzzy Zoeller, after making racially insensitive jokes

And avoid the near occasions of sin.

"I screwed up."—The Chicago Cubs' Sammy Sosa, caught with a corked bat.[11]

Be very suspicious of us when we claim that what the church once considered serious sin, we consider not so serious. The problem is not simply that we are soft on sin, but rather that we are soft on the notion of a forgiving God. Having lost the sense of a gracious God who has this thing for sinners, we can't dare admit and confess our sin, for what would we do with our confession except to feel depressed about our sin? Our God wants to hear about our sin, as honestly and ably as we are able to tell about it, in order to forgive our sin, in order that we might experience the full depth, the great height and breadth of God's love. Our God cares enough about us not only to name for us our sin as sin but also to relieve us of sin's burden.

In my wife's DISCIPLE class, a year-long series of Bible studies in which the class participants read straight through the Bible, there was that evening when they got to the book of Leviticus. A member of the group opened the discussion by saying, "I have been dreading this book ever since this month began. I had heard that Leviticus had some harsh things to say about people like me. As you may know, Leviticus doesn't approve of my sexual orientation. But then I read Leviticus, the whole of it. And I'll just say this. Leviticus is not only down on some of the things I do, it's down on just about everything! Leviticus really has a long list of abominable deeds."

Then someone else in the group asked, "Why does God care about all that? There's rules for how to prepare food, how to treat livestock, how to behave during menstruation. You would think God would have more to do than to monitor all that!"

Then another said, "I think it's sort of wonderful that we have a God who wants all of us, who cares about what we do in a bedroom or a boardroom, the living room and the kitchen, a God who wants us to show love, not only to one another, but even to animals in the barn. Our God wants it all."

So before you dismiss our God as being overly prudish in divine concern about our genitals, consider the glory of a God who, despite concern over war in the Middle East, famine in Africa, and systemic injustice right here at home, has time to worry even about something so relatively insignificant as sex, even to condemn Lust as a sin.

Still, is Lust so great a sin? I remind you of our opening thesis, namely, that the Seven are sins not so much because of our theories about human nature but rather because of the nature of God. Sexuality is one of the ways we express our love. And God in Jesus Christ appears to want to love us, and for us to love God in response, in the extreme.

I had my freshman seminar read Augustine's *Confessions*. Most of these modern young adults were mystified by Augustine's ancient account of his life and his journey toward God. "This guy seems obsessed with sex," said one student. "Man, he's got some real hang-ups about sex and seems to feel terribly guilty about his sexuality. What gives?"

Another responded, "I found the *Confessions* to be a very sensuous, even erotic work in places. Not erotic in the sense of men and women, but in the sense that Augustine feels that you ought not to have sex with anyone—unless it is God."

I might have put the matter a bit differently, but I like her insight and found it to be right on target. Augustine's story can be read as a sensuous man's search for God, and it can also be read as a sensuous God's search for a man. Our God, the one rendered in scripture, is no calm, cool bureaucrat, just following the rules, treating everyone dispassionately. Our God longs to make love to us, enjoys having us, in our own fumbling ways, make love to God. This God, out of love, gets rather worked up when we lust for other gods, when we squander our love elsewhere than upon the one "in whom we live, and move and have our being." As Augustine said, our hearts are created to be restless until they find rest in the proper object of their love. Again, as with some of the other Seven, the sin in Lust is not in the desire but rather in having an improper, false object of our desire. Christianity is not about extinguishing desire but rather about training in hungering and thirsting (lusting) after the One who has created us for communion with God's self.

As Meister Eckhart said, "Everything praises God. Darkness, privations, defects, and evil praise God and bless God."[12] Even our sins, even our carnal, unimaginative, animalistic sins such as Lust, in the majesty of God's grace, praise God and enable God to show the great things that can be done with petty, human-all-too-human sinners like us. Jesus Christ came to call (one more time, this time in unison) *sinners*. As a pastor, give me a lustful, seeking, reaching, desirous person in my congregation rather than a detached, cool, controlled, repressed apathetic person. It's easier to contain and direct a fire than it is to raise the dead.

We discuss the Seven not only honestly to point to them, but also in order to deal with them. The God who was able to raise the dead is able also to redeem sinners. Although I may not be able to extinguish the fire of Lust as it burns in me, I can dampen some of its flame. I can't do this by myself, but if Jesus can raise the dead he can surely deal with a little old thing like Lust. He came not only to receive and to forgive sinners but also to redeem sinners, to give us the means to conquer even something so utterly natural and congenial to our natures as Lust.

A while back a young man, a student, was telling me about being at a party with a group of friends, and one of his friends "came on" to him.

"But I sort of surprised myself when I said, 'No, that's not a good idea,'" he said. "I walked away feeling fairly good.

Overjoyed, even. I thought to myself, 'Gosh, I'm a better Christian than I thought!' I'm in a better church than I thought. My church has lots of problems, many shortcomings, but at least it's made a relatively faithful person out of a creep like me."

By the grace of God, a good-enough church, and lots of practice, it is possible even for ordinary folk like us to become saints.

POSTSCRIPT

On September 11, the Duke campus ministers met to decide how to respond to the deep pastoral needs of students on that fateful day. We decided to offer prayer for any who wanted to talk to God, or who were willing to listen to God, every day at noon in our chapel. A dozen or so showed up for the first couple of days to sit in a circle and pray, led by one of the campus ministers.

As Providence would have it, on the Friday of that fateful week, President Bush declared a day for the whole nation to pray. But the campus minister who was to lead the service at Duke that Friday at noon was the only person in the country who did not get the message that the President had ordered a day of prayer—perhaps because this particular campus minister is a Bible-thumping

Evangelical who listens more to Scripture than to government press releases. At any rate, he showed up in the chapel, expecting the usual dozen or so faithful, only to encounter a couple of thousand folk ready to do what the President ordered.

So this Bible-believing, conservative, evangelical, virtually fundamentalist campus minister simply went on as usual, saying, "Let us pray." He then led the assembly in a quarter-of-an-hour's confession of sin. He asked God to forgive us for our arrogance, our insensitivity to the needs of others, our trust in national weaponry more than God's power, and so on.

That afternoon my e-mails let me know that this was not the sort of chat with God that the congregation had in mind. People were mad. Many of the e-mails complained, "We came there hurting, grieving, and we got all this talk about sin." Others said, "We're victims, not sinners!"

I replied that the supervising minister was a conservative, evangelical, Bible-thumping pastor whereas I was not, but that did not seem to pacify them.

And yet, two days later, when on Sunday I summoned a couple of thousand to worship in Duke Chapel, and the organ played, and we sang an opening hymn of praise and comfort, what then did we do? I had everyone stand and repeat in unison, words to this effect: "We sin. We do wrong. We mess up. We worship false gods. We really don't believe that God is in charge of the world." And then I pronounced over them the complete forgiveness of that sin that was so publicly confessed.

I fear that Christians fail to appreciate how very strange we are in this matter of sin. There are those who think of prayer as asking God to do things for us—petition, intercession. There are those who think of prayer primarily as praise—let's all get together and just say nice things about God. Christians are strange in our conviction that prayer is also a time when we do things for God, when we lay ourselves open to the words and will of God, when we are honest about who we are and have failed to be. Prayer, specifically *Christian* prayer, is not for the faint of heart or the squeamish about their limitations. Prayer really isn't prayer "in Jesus' name" if it is never about confession of sin.

As I recall, President George W. Bush once was asked something like, "What are the greatest mistakes you have made in your administration of the nation? Is there anything you might have done differently?"

The President could think of nothing that he would have done differently. I found it sad that a person who is a Christian, a person who says that he prays a great deal, appeared to have so much trouble making the simple admission that "Yes, I messed up and I admit it." Perhaps the problem is that the President prays, but he does so alone, without the aid and prodding of the church. Perhaps if he attended church more often, he would get the hang of it. Like we said earlier, church is training in how to be a sinner.

As we have noted in this book, it is a major claim of the Christian faith that Jesus gives us the means to be honest about our condition. We are, by the grace of God, redeemed. But we are still sinners who are redeemed in, because of, and despite our sin. Let's all say it together just one more time: Jesus Christ came to seek and to save, to invite and to be in communion with, sinners.

Paradoxically, it is that sense of security in our redemption, coupled with a gracious honesty about our sin, that enables us to be more than we would have been if we had not been loved in our sin. I have found, as a pastoral counselor, that the most ineffective way to change someone's behavior is to say to them, "I am going to change your behavior." That doesn't work. Defenses arise, denial begins, and change is impossible.

A better way is to try to understand and relate to that person as he or she is, as someone caught in a web of self-destructive, hurtful sin and yet, in the Cross of Jesus, loved in their sin. They are saved as they are, not as we would like them to be. To be there with them, to listen to them, to show care and concern for them, as they are, is the necessary prelude to true transformation.

That's what God has done for us in Jesus Christ.

One of the great testimonials to the power of God in Jesus Christ to change people, to enable us to be more than we could have been without the love of Christ, is that you have spent all this time reading about sin! In a basically deceitful culture, ruled over by a President who can't think of one thing that he might have done differently if given a chance to do it over again, it is rather remarkable that you are able to think so much about your propensity to wander, stumble, actively rebel against, and deface the life that God intended for you. In a world like ours, it's a remarkable spiritual achievement to be able to read a book about sin without wanting to kill the author who wrote it!

But that "spiritual achievement" isn't yours. That achievement is Christ's. Jesus Christ, who said up front that he came to seek and to save the lost, seems to have found you, seems to have rather remarkably transformed a basically deceitful person like you into a sort of saint. This makes you a miracle, a surprising work of God.

Thus Martin Luther spoke of us as *simul iustis et peccator*—we are both justified (loved and accepted by God in Christ, redeemed and saved) and sinner (rebellious, deceitful, dishonorable) at the same time. Our sanctification isn't finished. God is still working on us, still transforming us, still holding up the mirror of truth to us and making us look at ourselves. We are yet learning to see ourselves as God sees us—mired in the muck of our sin and yet destined by God to stand up and shine as the blessed children of God. There is thus a necessary tension in the Christian life as we find ourselves stretched between two poles, having two natures, torn between two alternatives. Yet there is also the quiet conviction that gradually—day by day, little by little, decision by decision—God in Christ is leading us, coaxing us, sometimes dragging us kicking and screaming—home.

QUESTIONS FOR STUDY AND REFLECTION

CHAPTER 1: THINKING ABOUT SIN

1. How have you experienced the Seven Deadly Sins even in, especially in, a holy place like the church?
2. Are you surprised by some of the sins on the list of the Seven? Is there a sin that you would add to the list?
3. Do you agree with the notion that the Seven most often thrive within the most tightly knit communities?

CHAPTER 2: PRIDE

1. Do you think that Pride is such a terrible sin? Or is Pride something that we need more of?
2. In what ways is our sin too much of a good thing? too little? Can you think of a time in your life when one of your virtues became one of your vices?
3. Are religious people—those who try to do right and sometimes take great pride in the ability to do good—particularly susceptible to the sin of Pride?

CHAPTER 3: ENVY

1. How, in your own life, have you experienced Envy breeding when you are in close proximity to other people?
2. Do you think it possible for anyone to be truly free of Envy? How?
3. In what ways does Envy make the envious person sick?

CHAPTER 4: ANGER

1. How does our Anger tend to turn on us and hurt us more than we hurt the object of our Anger?
2. What do you think is the major difference between the sin of Anger and the virtue of righteous indignation against injustice?
3. How do you react to the biblical notion that Jesus at times got very angry? Have you heard much about that Jesus in church?

CHAPTER 5. SLOTH

1. Were you surprised to find that Sloth, or apathy, is a serious sin? Do you agree?

2. In what ways have you observed yourself or others failing to avail themselves of God's means of grace and thereby committing the sin of Sloth?

3. How might it be said that Sloth is a particular problem for modern Americans?

CHAPTER 6. GREED

1. If you were asked to vote for the one sin among the Seven that most afflicts contemporary Americans, would you vote for Greed? Why or why not?

2. Is there something about our consumer culture that encourages Greed? What, if anything, in the Christian church discourages Greed?

3. Are you guilty of Greed? How might someone else—say, someone who was intent on nailing you as a full-fledged sinner—challenge you on your answer?

CHAPTER 7. GLUTTONY

1. Really now, is Gluttony such a terrible sin? Give reasons for your response.

2. What do you think of the historic view that Gluttony was not simply eating too much but also consuming "too daintily"?

3. Of all the Seven, Gluttony seems to be the sin that modern folk abhor. What is your view of our widespread revulsion of Gluttony?

CHAPTER 8. LUST

1. What makes our passion a good thing or a bad thing?
2. In what ways does our culture make it difficult for us to think about our sexual desire—which so often leads us into Lust—in a Christian way?
3. Is Jesus being prudish to make such a big deal out of our all-too-human propensity to Lust?
4. In what ways does the church enable us to critique that which the world regards as "all-too-human"?

POSTSCRIPT

1. What do you now think of the author's assertion that the church is "training in how to be a sinner"?
2. How does a gracious Savior like Jesus enable us not only to be honest about our sin but also to become better people despite our sin?
3. In what ways might it be sinful to write or read a book about the Seven Deadly Sins?

NOTES

INTRODUCTION

1. C. S. Lewis, as quoted in *Mephistopheles: The Devil in the Modern World*, by Jeffrey Burton Russell (Ithaca, NY: Cornell University Press, 1986), 80.

2. See Carl E. Braaten and Robert W. Jenson eds., *Sin, Death, and the Devil* (Grand Rapids: Eerdmans, 2000).

3. One of the purposes of Reinhold Niebuhr's *Nature and Destiny of Man* (New York: Scribner, 1964) was "to relate the biblical and distinctively Christian conception of sin as pride and self-love to the observable behavior of men." For Niebuhr, sin is a universal attribute that all people display as a result of their awareness of their finitude. Feminists have criticized Niebuhr's view of sin as culture-bound, perhaps gender-determined rather than biblically derived. See particularly Judith

Plaskow, *Sex, Sin, and Grace: Women's Experience and the Theologies of Reinhold Niebuhr and Paul Tillich* (Washington, DC: University Press of America, 1980), 62-72.

4. Karl Barth, *Dogmatics in Outline* (New York: Harper, 1959), 151.

5. James William McClendon, Jr., "Sin," in *A New Handbook of Christian Theology*, ed. D. W. Musser and J. L. Price (Nashville: Abingdon Press, 1992), 446-47.

6. See *Sighing for Eden: Sin and Evil in the Christian Life* (Nashville: Abingdon Press, 1985) for my thoughts on the implications of a doctrine of original sin for the practice of Christian ministry (pp. 183-90).

7. Alvin Redman, *Oscar Wilde Epigrams: An Anthology* (New York: Day, 1956), 74.

8. M. Scott Peck, *People of the Lie: The Hope for Healing Evil* (New York: Simon and Schuster, 1983), 263.

9. Ibid.

1. THINKING ABOUT SIN

1. William H. Willimon, *Sighing for Eden: Sin and Evil in the Christian Life* (Nashville: Abingdon Press, 1985).

2. This is from the essay by Don Herzog, "Envy," in *Wicked Pleasures: Meditations on the Seven "Deadly" Sins*, ed. Robert C. Solomon (Lanham, MD: Rowman & Littlefield, 1999).

3. Matthew Fox, *Sins of the Spirit, Blessings of the Flesh* (New York: Harmony Books, 1999), 73.

2. PRIDE

1. Bertrand Russell, as quoted in *The Harper Book of Quotations*, 3rd ed., ed. Robert I. Fitzhenry (New York: HarperPerennial, 1993), 372.

2. Richard H. Thaler, *The Winner's Curse: Paradoxes and Anomalies of*

Economic Life (Princeton, NJ: Princeton University Press, 1992).

3. J. D. Salinger, as quoted in *Harper Book of Quotations*, 372.

4. Martin Buber, *Good and Evil, Two Interpretations* (New York: Scribner, 1953), 64.

3. ENVY

1. I have been greatly helped in my thoughts on Envy by the wonderful little book of Joseph Epstein, *Envy* (New York: Oxford University Press, 2003).

2. David Hume, *A Treatise of Human Nature*, 2nd ed., ed. L. A. Selby-Bigge, rev. P. H. Nidditch (Oxford: Clarendon Press, 1978), 377.

3. Sir Philip Sidney, *The Countess of Pembroke's Arcadia* (1590}, ed. Maurice Evans (Harmondsworth: Penguin, 1984), 620.

4. Ibid., quoted by Epstein, *Envy*, xxi, quoted by Leslie Farber.

5. Don Herzog, "Envy," in *Wicked Pleasures: Meditations on the Seven "Deadly" Sins*, ed. Robert C. Solomon (Lanham, MD: Rowman & Littlefield, 1999), 151.

6. Ibid., 149.

7. Ibid., 156.

4. ANGER

1. Martin Luther, in *The Harper Book of Quotations*, 3rd ed., ed. Robert I. Fitzhenry (New York: HarperPerennial, 1993), 36.

2. Phyllis Diller, in ibid, 36.

5. SLOTH

1. I have been aided in these thoughts by the chapter "Sloth" by Thomas Pynchon in *Wicked Pleasures: Meditations on the Seven "Deadly"*

logy, Vol.

Sins, ed. Robert C. Solomon (Lanham, MD: Rowman & Littlefield, 1999), 81-86.

2. Although Paulsen lost that election, he seems to have captured the hearts of American voters. In the 2002 presidential election, according to a TV newscast, only 35 percent of voters cast ballots.

3. Saint Thomas Aquinas, *Summa Theologiæ*, Vol. XXXV (New York: McGraw-Hill Book Company in conjunction with the Blackfriars, 1972), 21. 2a.2æ. Q. 35. art 1.

4. Ibid., p. 23. 2a.2æ. Q. 35. art. 1.

5. Owen Chadwick, ed., *Western Asceticism: Selected Translation with Introductions and Notes*, Vol. 12, The Library of Christian Classics (Philadelphia: Westminster Press, 1958), 212-13.

6. "Appendix I" to St. Thomas Aquinas, *Summa Theologiæ*, Vol. XXXV, pp. 189-91. 2a2æ. Q. 35.

7. Matthew Fox, *Original Blessing* (Santa Fe, NM: Bear, 1983), 169.

8. Ibid., 141.

9. Aquinas, *Summa Theologiæ*, Vol. XXXV, p. 25. 2a.2æ. Q. 35. art. 1.

10. Henry Adams, *The Education of Henry Adams* (New York: The Modern Library, 1931), 34.

11. Jonathan Franzen, "Perchance to Dream: In the Age of Images, a Reason to Write Novels," *Harpers* (April 1996): 53.

12. In my analysis of Updike's novel, I have been helped by Ralph Wood's insightful article "Into the Void: Updike's Sloth and America's Religion," *The Christian Century* (24 April 1996): 452-57.

13. Ibid., 457.

14. William R. May, *A Catalogue of Sins*, as quoted by Ralph C. Wood, "Into the Void," 617.

15. Fox, *Original Blessing*, 146.

6. GREED

1. Charles Dickens, A *Christmas Carol* (Garden City, NY: Doubleday, 1965).

2. James Ogilvy, "Greed" in *Wicked Pleasures: Meditations on the Seven "Deadly" Sins*, ed. Robert C. Solomon (Lanham, MD: Rowman & Littlefield, 1999).

3. Matthew Fox, *Original Blessing* (Santa Fe, NM: Bear, 1983).

4. Karl Barth, *Church Dogmatics*, Vol. III.

7. GLUTTONY

1. Saint Thomas Aquinas, *Summa Theologiæ*, Vol. 43 (New York: McGraw-Hill Book Company in conjunction with the Blackfriars, 1972), 17. 2a.2æ. Q. 142. art. 4.

2. Geoffrey Chaucer, "The Pardoner's Tale," in *The Canterbury Tales*, trans. Nevill Coghill (New York: Penguin Books, 1951), 59.

3. Aristotle, *The Nicomachean Ethics*, trans. David Ross (New York: Oxford University Press, 1998), 29.

4. Francine Prose, *Gluttony*, The Seven Deadly Sins series (New York: Oxford University Press, 2003), 12.

5. Ibid., 27.

6. Augustine, *On Christian Doctrine*, trans. D. W. Robertson (New York: Liberal Arts Press, 1958).

7. Prose, *Gluttony*, 14.

8. Ibid., 19.

9. William Ian Miller, "Gluttony," in *Wicked Pleasures: Meditations on the Seven "Deadly" Sins*, ed. Robert C. Solomon (Lanham, MD: Rowman & Littlefield, 1999), 30

10. Ibid., 34.

11. Aquinas, *Summa Theologiæ*, Vol. XLIII, p. 147, 2a2æ. Q. 150. art. 1.
12. Prose, *Gluttony*, 77-78.
13. Ibid., 10. I thoroughly enjoyed Prose's insights on Gluttony and have used many of them in this chapter.
14. Ibid., 11.
15. Aquinas, *Summa Theologiæ*, Vol. XLII, p. 47. 2a2æ. Q. 142. art. 4.

8. LUST

1. C. S. Lewis, *Mere Christianity* (San Francisco: HarperSanFrancisco, 2001), 94-95.
2. Taken from footnote a. to St. Thomas Aquinas, *Summa Theologiæ*, Vol. XLIII (New York: McGraw-Hill in conjunction with the Blackfriars, 1972), p. 188. 2a2æ. Q. 142. art. 4.
3. Mae West in *I'm No Angel*, 1933.
4. M. D. O'Connor, *Parabola: Myth and the Quest for Meaning*, "The Seven Deadly Sins," Vol. X, #4, (November 1989).
5. Aquinas, *Summa Theologiæ*, Quest. 167. art. 2.
6. Oscar Wilde, *In Conversation*, as quoted in *The Harper Book of Quotations*, 3rd ed., ed. Robert I. Fitzhenry (New York: Harper Perennial, 1993), 149.
7. Raymond Bernard Blakney, *Meister Eckhart: A Modern Translation* (New York: Harper and Bros., 1941), 59.
8. Aquinas, *Summa Theologiæ*, Vol. XLIII, p. 225. 2a2æ. Q. 154. art. 2.
9. Ibid.
10. Ibid., p. 207. 2a2æ. Q. 154. art. 1.
11. Martin E. Marty, *Christian Century* (10 February 2004): 47.
12. Matthew Fox, *Original Blessing* (Santa Fe, NM: Bear, 1983), 529.

CPSIA information can be obtained at www.ICGtesting.com
Printed in the USA
LVOW07s2220260116

471848LV00002B/19/P